LET IT GO

LET IT GO

Come Home from Your
GUILT TRIP

MARK ATTEBERRY

Standard® PUBLISHING

Cincinnati, Ohio

Published by Standard Publishing, Cincinnati, Ohio
www.standardpub.com

Printed in: United States of America
Substantive editor: Diane Stortz
Project editor: Lynn Lusby Pratt
Cover design: Rex Bonomelli
Interior design: Dorcas Design & Typesetting

Published in association with the literary agency of Alive Communications, Inc., 7680 Goddard Street, Suite 200, Colorado Springs, Colorado 80920, www.alivecommunications.com.

ISBN 978-0-7847-2364-7

Library of Congress Cataloging-in-Publication Data

Atteberry, Mark.
  Let it go : come home from your guilt trip / Mark Atteberry.
     p. cm.
  Includes bibliographical references.
  ISBN 978-0-7847-2364-7
  1. Guilt--Religious aspects--Christianity. 2. Forgiveness of sin--Religious aspects--Christianity.
3. Forgiveness--Religious aspects--Christianity. I. Title.
  BT722.A88 2010
  234'.5--dc22
                                2009050490

15 14 13 12 11 10   1 2 3 4 5 6 7 8 9

For David and Cherita Beehn

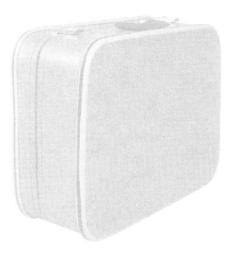

May the LORD bless you and protect you.

May the LORD smile on you and be gracious to you.

May the LORD show you his favor and give you his peace.

—Numbers 6:24-26

CONTENTS

ACKNOWLEDGMENTS

Have you ever felt like an imposter? Like you are the one person in your peer group who doesn't belong? I experience this every time I see a new book of mine in print. Part of this stems from my struggle with inferiority, which I document in this book. Another part has to do with my admiration for so many other writers. But a big part comes from the fact that I know how many fantastic people had a hand in the finished product.

If you only knew how hard Lee Hough works to negotiate my book deals. If you could just see the folks at Standard Publishing—Dale Reeves, Lindsay Black, Sarah Felkey, and others—brainstorming on how my idea just might work. And, oh yes, if you could see my editors, Diane Stortz and Lynn Pratt, hunched over their computers, faces scrunched up, trying to untangle my participles, you'd know what I mean. These people keep me from embarrassing myself, and I am deeply grateful to all of them.

I am also indebted to my wife, Marilyn, for her constant love and devotion. It's not easy being married to a writer. Our minds are often elsewhere, our spare time is often spent in front of the computer, and our many frustrations often make us irritable. Marilyn puts up with all of this and somehow manages to maintain her good humor.

Finally, I am thankful for my readers. You keep buying my books and sending me wonderful e-mails. Time and time again you make my day with a note of encouragement, and it's amazing how often those come on days when inferiority and I are having a good scrap. Thank you for being in my corner. You make me want to keep plugging away.

‖‖‖‖‖ INTRODUCTION ‖‖‖‖‖

DID JESUS HAVE LOVE HANDLES (AND DOES HE CARE IF I DO)?

A book idea can hit you anytime. This one came at lunch.

I went to a well-known seafood restaurant to meet an even better-known health and fitness expert. The man is a best-selling author and all-around good guy. I like him a lot. But I couldn't have been more uncomfortable if I'd had fire ants in my underwear.

My discomfort started the moment he walked in wearing a skintight T-shirt stretched over his chiseled six-pack abs and tucked into the twenty-nine-inch waistband of his slacks. I with my love handles stood to greet him and winced at the crushing force of his handshake. It was all I could do to keep from crying out in pain.

But things got worse.

I had my eye on a pasta and shrimp entrée smothered in creamy alfredo sauce—until Mr. Flat Belly ordered baked fish and broccoli, even stipulating to the waitress that he wanted no butter or seasoning of any kind on his food. With my self-image suddenly in full plummet mode, I quickly abandoned my pasta dream and muttered, "Uh, I'll have the same thing."

It was the worst-tasting meal I've ever eaten. Dry. Bland. And made even drier and blander by the fact that a lady sitting at the table next to us was eating my shrimp pasta.

Could things get any worse? Oh yes.

As we chatted, my friend talked about his health regimen. I wasn't completely clueless about health regimens, but I'd never heard of one like his, involving a strenuous two-hour workout every day. No doubt I could have asked countless intelligent questions about exercise or metabolism, but I opted for, "How many push-ups can you do?" He didn't know, because he usually stops at one hundred. I, who couldn't do ten push-ups if an al Qaeda terrorist held a gun to my head, nodded as if I completely understood.

Driving back to my office after lunch, I thought, *I am a pitiful excuse for a human being.* There I sat, wearing expandable-waistband pants to accommodate my paunch, yet feeling irritated that I didn't get my pasta. And while I was heading to my office to park myself in front of my computer (well within reach of my candy dish), my friend was making a beeline to his home gym to bench-press small cars and ride a thousand miles on his stationary bike.

I felt like a slug.

But then I began to wonder . . .

> **Driving back to my office after lunch, I thought, *I am a pitiful excuse for a human being.***

- Did Jesus have love handles?
- Does he care if I do?
- Does he see the expandable waistband of my pants as some kind of moral failure?
- Could it be that some of us weren't meant to look like we just stepped out of a Soloflex commercial?
- Was I being too hard on myself?
- Did my concepts of righteousness and God need to be overhauled?
- Will there be cheese fries in Heaven?

Ultimately, I answered these questions: probably not, no, no, yes, probably, without a doubt, and I sure hope so.

Then I decided to do three things:

1. Let it go.

2. Come home from my guilt trip once and for all.

3. Try to help other frustrated people like me do the same.

You are now holding the fruit of those decisions. This book is not—I repeat, it is *not*—a condemnation of all things related to self-discipline. I believe in self-discipline. In my home office I have dumbbells and a stationary bike that I fully intend to use someday. Rather, this book is a plea for those of us with love handles (and other imperfections) to stop beating ourselves up. I'm convinced that we listen far too much to our accuser and far too little to our Redeemer. Consequently, we forget what God never forgets: that we are made of dust (Psalm 103:14). We forget that while man looks at the outward appearance, God looks at the heart (1 Samuel 16:7). We forget that Jesus came to save us, not judge us (John 3:17). Worst of all, we forget that we are saved by grace, not goodness (Ephesians 2:8, 9).

I hate to admit it, but this has been my struggle for as long as I can remember. I have wrestled with perfectionism, guilt, and inferiority as if they were pit bulls chewing on my ankles. Of course I know about God's grace. I can quote the Scriptures about grace frontward and backward. I even have some dandy little sermons on grace in my file. But I have rarely allowed myself to *enjoy* God's grace, because I've been too busy believing I should be a better person than I am.

Sound familiar? If so, this book is for you.

My goal is not to make you feel good about your love handles or to encourage you to order pasta and alfredo indiscriminately. Self-discipline and sacrifice are admirable virtues. Maybe you *do* need to be doing better in some areas. I simply want to remind you that the God we serve is not a cruel taskmaster and that he has created all things (including the ingredients for a killer alfredo sauce) for us to enjoy (1 Timothy 6:17). I want to convince you that your weaknesses and imperfections, while they may need attention, are no match for his grace (1 John 1:9; Hebrews 4:16). I want to help you gain a new appreciation of his

> **The God we serve is not a cruel taskmaster.**

love so you can stop feeling like a miserable creep and start acting like the precious son or daughter you are (Romans 8:15). And I want to challenge the assertions of modern-day Pharisees who want you to believe that any activity with an element of pleasure in it is a sin.

In a nutshell, I want to help you rediscover the joy of your salvation.

All of my books have theme verses. For this one I have chosen the blessing that God instructed Aaron to give to the people of Israel: "May the LORD bless you and protect you. May the LORD smile on you and be gracious to you. May the LORD show you his favor and give you his peace" (Numbers 6:24-26).

I like to think of this blessing as God's self-portrait. Like an artist with a full palette of colors, he could have chosen any words to describe himself. He could have tossed out a couple of lightning bolts to punctuate a red-hot "sinners in the hands of an angry God" kind of speech. But no, he chose the softest, gentlest, sweetest words imaginable. He obviously wants his people to see him as a smiling, gracious, peace-giving God.

Why? Because that's exactly who he is.

If you have allowed perfectionism, guilt, and inferiority to cloud this life-transforming truth, I hope you'll keep reading. You've been on your guilt trip long enough. Whatever unwarranted self-infliction has been making you miserable, it's time to let it go, turn around, and head for home.

IT'S TIME TO COME HOME

I felt guilty. I thought for some reason . . . I was alive and Buddy and those boys were dead, and I didn't know how, but somehow I'd caused it.

—*Waylon Jennings*

Guilt. I believe there's no worse feeling a human can experience.

The English poet Nicholas Rowe called guilt an avenging fiend that follows behind us with a whip. William Wordsworth said that from a single guilty deed "a thousand . . . haunting thoughts proceed." And the Roman playwright Seneca observed that "every guilty person is his own hangman."[1]

Makes you think of Judas, doesn't it? He was so tortured by guilt after he betrayed our Lord that he did indeed become his own hangman (Matthew 27:5). And King David, though he didn't slide a noose around his neck and jump from a tree limb, certainly knew what it was like to be stalked by Nicholas Rowe's whip-wielding fiend. After his affair with Bathsheba, David wrote, "I recognize my rebellion; it haunts me day and night" (Psalm 51:3).

I need to point out that guilt, although unpleasant, can be both well deserved and helpful. When we've sinned and we need to apologize, make restitution, or undertake wholesale changes to our behavior, the crack of a whip across the back can provide just the motivation we need to get on with it. The apostle Paul acknowledged this when he said, "The kind of sorrow God wants us to experience leads us away from sin and results in salvation" (2 Corinthians 7:10). I have benefited from this kind of godly sorrow many times and am truly thankful for it. As far as I'm concerned, anything that steers my drifting soul back toward obedience and a healthy relationship with God is a good thing.

However, not everybody who feels guilty *should*. In fact, if my experience as a pastor is any indication, I'd say it would be easier to find a unicorn grazing in a cow pasture than to find a Christian who's never been on a guilt trip. For over thirty years I've watched a steady parade of slump-shouldered believers stagger into my office, collapse on the couch, and burst into tears—over situations in which they ultimately had no involvement or responsibility or over mistakes and imperfections they had greatly overblown. I find that even when they *have* sinned, they often are still punishing themselves for what God has long since forgiven and forgotten.

How does this happen?

YOUR GUILT-TRIP TRAVEL AGENT

Ultimately, Satan is behind every guilt trip. That's why the Bible calls him "the accuser" (Revelation 12:10). He looks into the life of every believer for little cracks where he can slip in evil insinuations that will grow and fester. And he doesn't pick on just the pitiful and pathetic. He loves to go after faith superstars too.

A good example is Satan's allegation against Job. The Bible says Job was "a man of complete integrity. He feared God and stayed away from evil" (Job 1:1). Yet Satan found a way to turn Job's righteousness into an accusation: he claimed that Job was only behaving himself for the benefits. "Take away everything he has, and he will surely curse you to your face!" Satan said to God (v. 11).

And so it goes.

There's no one so good that Satan can't find an accusation to throw in his face. It's his specialty. And he triggers these accusations several ways.

Comparison

In the introduction of this book, I told about the time I had lunch with a well-known health and fitness expert. I walked away from that encounter experiencing guilt, but it wasn't because he had cruelly pointed out my shortcomings. He had not said or done anything like that. I simply couldn't quit thinking about how far above and beyond me he'd managed to grow in the area of self-discipline. His V-shaped torso reminded me of all the times I'd promised—and failed—to start working out and to lay off the French fries. In his presence the ten extra pounds I carry around my middle seemed like thirty. And seeing him relish his plain fish and broccoli while I was choking down mine with huge gulps of water (instead of the sweet tea I would have ordered if he hadn't been there) just accentuated my weakness.

Let's face it. Seeing your failure next to somebody else's success can be painful. Like when the neighbor kid lands a scholarship to Stanford and your kid is caught shoplifting at the local 7-Eleven . . . or when the church across town is running in the thousands and the church you lead can't even break two hundred . . . or when the couple next door is jetting off to Hawaii for a second honeymoon and you're being served with divorce papers.

Oh, but Satan loves it! Our accuser is never happier than when he has a chance to point at somebody more successful than we are and say, "See, that's what *your* life would be like if you weren't such a miserable excuse for a human being!"

Catastrophe

Satan also uses catastrophe to trigger accusations against us. Just let something bad happen, and he'll find a way to make you believe you're responsible, even when you're not.

If your husband is caught cheating, Satan will tell you it never would have happened if you'd been a better wife. If your friend commits suicide, he'll remind you of a hundred occasions when you could have offered some help or encouragement but didn't. Or if your business goes belly-up, he'll assure you that only a moron could mess up such a golden opportunity.

On February 3, 1959, a small plane carrying Buddy Holly and his band crashed on its way to Fargo, North Dakota.[2] A young Waylon

Jennings was a member of that band and gave up his seat at the last minute to J. P. Richardson, otherwise known as the Big Bopper. As the quote at the beginning of this chapter indicates, Jennings experienced tremendous guilt feelings after the crash, even though he'd had nothing to do with the plane going down.

A few years ago Marilyn and I were vacationing in St. Louis when a nasty hurricane ripped through the area where we live in central Florida. We had planned our vacation months ahead of time and couldn't possibly have known that a major storm would materialize that very week. I remember experiencing incredible guilt as I watched the storm reports in a restaurant more than a thousand miles away from the howling winds. Why wasn't I there, riding out the storm with my friends, ready to minister if needed? I could almost hear Satan saying, "How dare you sit here munching on nachos while your friends are fighting for their lives!" I wasn't guilty of anything, but I *felt* guilty. Satan's accusations can overwhelm logic and reason. You've got to hand it to him—he's good at what he does.

> **I wasn't guilty of anything, but I *felt* guilty.**

Confusion

Sometimes bad things happen that are a mystery. They defy explanation, which is a green light for Satan to move in and start whispering in your ear.

For example, I've been the pastor of Poinciana Christian Church since 1989, but in the early '90s I almost quit because of a confusion-induced guilt trip. For some reason, after a period of growth, the church started going in reverse. Attendance and offerings dropped, morale sank as a result, but the elders and I looked at our ministry from every angle and couldn't pin down a single reason for the decline. We were totally confused.

And that's when Satan went to work on me.

In my spirit I heard him say, "The buck stops with you, buddy. You're the leader of this outfit. If it isn't working, it must be your fault. Look at that growing church on the other side of town. Now there's a *real* preacher. *That* man knows what he's doing. Unlike you, *he* knows how to motivate and lead people. Good grief, man. If you stay here another year, you'll kill the church completely!"

Time has proven those thoughts to be untrue, but they were my reality at that time. Satan relentlessly attacked my spirit, and I believed him. Surely everything was my fault!

We all encounter confusing circumstances in life. When your spouse seems distant and you don't know why, when your child's grades drop and you don't know why, when you miss out on a big promotion and you don't know why—you can count on Satan to show up at those moments with a big ol' club aimed at your head.

Criticism

I'll devote an entire chapter to criticism later in the book, but I need to mention it here too.

Satan employs an army of critics and sometimes finds his most accomplished ones among God's own people. The late author Mike Yaconelli said, "When Jesus and his followers show up, it isn't long before people start pointing fingers and calling names. Jesus was called all kinds of names: wine-bibber (what is a wine-bibber, anyway?), Sabbath breaker, blasphemer. Over the centuries, religious people have refined name-calling to an art. The name most commonly used today? *Unspiritual!*"[3]

Sometimes referred to as the morality police or God's gestapo, these religious name callers believe they've been ordained by God to sniff out and expose unspirituality wherever it hides. Not only are they outrageously self-righteous and arrogant, they've defined the word *unspiritual* so broadly that just about everything except prayer and fasting turns out to be a sin. These holier-than-thou types would never guess in a million years that they are some of Satan's favorites.

Do you remember Dana Carvey's Church Lady character from *Saturday Night Live*? ("How *conveeenient!*") A caricature of the kind of people I'm referring to, Church Lady ranted in one skit about the sinfulness of Santa Claus, even rearranging the word *Santa* to spell *Satan.* ("Well, isn't that special!") In another, she chastised a young woman for bringing cherry Jell-O to the church potluck because, as everyone knows, red is *someone's* favorite color. ("Could it be . . . *Satan*?")

I'll admit that I think the Church Lady is hilarious. But I also know there are real people who are almost that narrow-minded and judgmental, and encountering them never makes us laugh. They pick you apart, criticize your every move, and make you feel terrible whether you deserve to or not. David described them perfectly: "They sharpen their tongues like swords and aim their bitter words like arrows. They shoot from ambush at the innocent, attacking suddenly and fearlessly" (Psalm 64:3, 4).

While I'm on the subject of criticism, I want to acknowledge that it's not always mouthy, holier-than-thou churchgoers, classmates, or coworkers who "aim their bitter words like arrows." Sometimes it's our own parents. Many children are raised in environments with unreasonable expectations and severe consequences for not measuring up. Harsh, critical parents might have good intentions, just as the intentions of the Church Lady and her cohorts are ultimately noble. Nevertheless, the damage their critical words inflict can be life altering. It's never surprising when the children of demanding, unreasonable parents fight a lifelong battle with guilt and inferiority.

I hope you can see that your guilt-trip travel agent has no shortage of ways to send you packing. The question is, Why is he so diligent in this effort? With so many potential serial killers, pornographers, and despots he could be grooming for worldwide influence, why does he bother with little ol' you and me?

Your Guilt-Trip Destination

The answer is in Proverbs 17:22: "A cheerful heart is good medicine, but a broken spirit saps a person's strength." We love the front half of that verse. You'll see it printed on everything from key chains to coffee mugs. Every preacher worth his salt has used it to kick off a sermon on joy, and rightfully so. A cheerful heart really *is* good medicine.

But while we're fawning over the front half of that verse, Satan locks in on the back half . . . the part we seldom notice. He knows that if he can break our spirits, he can sap our strength. And if he can sap our strength, he stands a much better chance of bringing us down.

This is where Satan's passion for the guilt trip is exposed. He knows that nothing breaks a believer's spirit like guilt. When we suffer from guilt, we feel far from God—ashamed, weak, dirty, unworthy of God's favor, and therefore reluctant to pray and ask for his help. In other words, we end up in a place of weakness and vulnerability.

David describes this awful place very vividly in Psalm 38:4-8: "My guilt overwhelms me—it is a burden too heavy to bear. My wounds fester and stink because of my foolish sins. I am bent over and racked with pain. All day long I walk around filled with grief. A raging fever burns within me, and my health is broken. I am exhausted and completely crushed. My groans come from an anguished heart."

If you're in the ugly and dangerous pit of guilt right now, you must give some serious thought to how you got there. If it's truly because of sin, you must confess and repent (1 John 1:8, 9). But if it's simply because Satan has sent you off on a guilt trip, embrace that reality and make up your mind that it's time to come home.

Your Guilt-Trip Return Ticket

Coming home from a guilt trip involves some activity, but most of it is going to take place between your ears. As I've pointed out, Satan poisons our thoughts to send us off on a guilt trip. We have to purify our thoughts if we want to come home. Here are some realities you can embrace that will clean up your mind and bring you back to the place of joy and peace where God intends for you to live.

> Coming home from a guilt trip involves some activity, but most of it is going to take place between your ears.

God Knows the Truth About You

Your friends and neighbors might not know the real you. Satan may cloud their minds and use them to hammer you with accusations. But don't think for a moment that God could ever be hoodwinked. If you're innocent, he knows it.

This is illustrated in John 12, where we find Jesus having dinner in Bethany with some of his closest friends and most loyal supporters.

Among those gathered around the table were Simon, a man with leprosy whom Jesus had healed (Mark 14:3); Lazarus, a dead man he raised; Mary, a dear friend who loved to sit at his feet and soak up his wisdom; and the disciples. Mary turned the evening on its ear by breaking open a jar of expensive perfume and anointing Jesus' feet.

In the eyes of the other guests, Mary's actions presented two problems. First, Mary had no business assuming such a prominent role in the evening's proceedings. She clearly breached etiquette in a culture where women were supposed to lay low and keep quiet. Second, the outrageously expensive perfume cost a small fortune. The *New Living Translation* says it was worth "a year's wages" (John 12:5).

Naturally, Judas spoke first. He went after Mary for her lack of judgment like a lion goes after a chunk of raw meat. How dare she be so thoughtless and wasteful!

But suddenly Jesus spoke up. I hear him with a booming voice— "Leave her alone!" (v. 7).

I can just imagine Judas's eyes popping open and his mouth snapping shut in midsentence. I picture him hanging his head and seething on the inside as Jesus explained in no uncertain terms that Mary had done nothing wrong.

We guilt-trip travelers need to see the clarity with which Jesus assessed the situation. All the men around that table may have been nodding in agreement with Judas. They probably all saw the logic of the indictment Judas pronounced on Mary. But Jesus knew she was innocent. He knows you're innocent too, if indeed you are. It doesn't matter how many people say otherwise.

If you're on a guilt trip, realizing that God knows the truth about you is the first big step you can take in the direction of home. It is so liberating to understand that the only one whose opinion actually matters is on your side.

The only one whose opinion actually matters is on your side.

You Are Called to Be a Disciple, Not a Clone

Matthew 28:19 does *not* say, "Go and make clones of all the nations, baptizing them in the name of the Father and the Son and the Holy Spirit." What Jesus *did* say is that we should make disciples. A disciple is a follower, period, which means that disciples can come in all shapes, sizes, and colors. A flat-bellied health and fitness expert can be a disciple, but so can a paunchy middle-aged preacher wearing expandable-waistband slacks. A seminary professor can be a disciple, but so can a brand-new Christian who doesn't know John 3:16 from the Gettysburg Address. A movie star who makes ten figures can be a disciple, but so can a homeless person who sleeps under a bridge.

You can give up playing the comparison game. You can quit trying to measure up to someone else and start finding your joy in that unique little DNA strand God gave to *you*. This is what Paul was getting at in 1 Corinthians 12 when he wrote about the body of Christ and its many unique members. The foot, the ear, and the eye all look completely different and accomplish different things, but they're all vital. "How strange a body would be if it had only one part!" Paul says (v. 19). Yes, and what a strange thing the church would be if everybody looked, acted, and thought exactly the same.

The next time you find yourself with guilt feelings because you don't think you compare favorably to some highfalutin believer, remember that there are people like you *he* will never be able to influence and people like him *you* will never be able to influence. This is the truth that always seems to escape us when we fall into the comparison trap: our diversity is a strength, not a weakness!

The Best Defense Against Criticism Is Faithfulness

Remember this; it's important: when critics howl your name unfairly, just keep plugging away. Don't quit. Don't argue. Don't try to placate. Keep going. Your faithfulness will eventually vindicate you.

Moses learned this lesson as he led the Israelites on their forty-year trek through the wilderness. Probably no one has ever been unfairly criticized more than Moses was during that time. And it wasn't just ordinary people who were on his case. Numbers 12 tells us that even Aaron and Miriam, Moses' brother and sister, got into the act. Eventually, Moses faced a plot to overthrow him (Numbers 14:4).

But Moses stayed the course. He remained faithful. He trusted God and just kept plugging, and he outlasted his critics. Today we revere him as one of the greatest heroes of the Bible, while those who tried to tear him down are long forgotten.

Please read the next paragraph very carefully.

The reason you must not counterattack when you are criticized is that you will almost certainly go too far. You will let your anger get the best of you. You will say or do too much, and then you *will* have something to feel guilty about. The whole point is to get home from your guilt trip guilt free. You do that by just being faithful. Romans 12:21 says, "Don't let evil conquer you, but conquer evil by doing good."

Oh, and as for your critics—if they need to be dealt with, God will take care of them: "'I will take revenge; I will pay them back,' says the LORD" (v. 19).

No Matter How Awful You Feel, You Can Choose Joy

If these words from Habakkuk 3:17, 18 are not underlined or highlighted in your Bible, they should be: "Even though the fig trees have no blossoms, and there are no grapes on the vines; even though the olive crop fails, and the fields lie empty and barren; even though the flocks die in the fields, and the cattle barns are empty, yet I will rejoice in the LORD! I will be joyful in the God of my salvation!"

When we *feel* guilty we often *act* guilty, even if we know deep down that we're not. We let that noxious mixture of guilt and inferiority settle over us like a cloud to darken everything we do . . . and the world responds accordingly. It's as if we're walking around with a sign that says, "I'm a sad excuse for a human being. Please kick me." The world is happy to oblige.

But it doesn't have to be that way. We can choose joy.

Author and physician Mike Mason said, "I haven't the slightest doubt that God is bending over backward all day long to give me joy—but I must take it. Jesus stands at the crossroads pointing the way to joy, inviting and encouraging, but I must choose. Lasting happiness comes only through choice, through the making of countless small decisions, one day at a time. Once I see this, it's not hard to choose. The hard part is admitting I have a choice."[4]

He's right. Even if the circumstances of your life are difficult and the know-it-alls are using you for target practice, there's nothing to stop you from placing your trust in God, putting a smile on your face, and being happy. The truth is that the sooner you start acting like you've come home from your guilt trip, the sooner you'll discover that you have.

> The sooner you start acting like you've come home from your guilt trip, the sooner you'll discover that you have.

You Will Find the Strength to Do All This in God, Not in Yourself

I know that not striking back at your critics and choosing joy when you think you're scum may seem to be undoable. But they're not.

David could give one whale of a testimony on this point.

In 1 Samuel 30, Ziklag was home base for David and his men, the place they had left their wives and children when they went to fight a battle. David and his six-hundred-man militia returned to Ziklag from one such battle with the heightened sense of anticipation that returning soldiers get, expecting to crest the hill and see their wives and children drop everything and run out to meet them. Instead, David and his men found the entire village burned to the ground. While they were gone, an Amalekite raiding party had swept in and taken everything, including their families.

The Bible says the men "wept until they could weep no more" (v. 4).

And then they got mad. Not at the Amalekites but at David.

Imagine David's emotions when he lost his wives and children and then his men blamed him for letting it happen. Verse 6 says, "They began to talk of stoning him." Something tells me that David would have helped them! Surely, as the one calling the shots, he felt responsible for leaving their wives and children defenseless—a colossal, inexcusable error. If ever a man carried a load of guilt, it was David at this moment.

"But David found strength in the LORD his God." That's the testimony of verse 6.

David could have folded the proverbial tent right there. He could have voluntarily stepped down in response to the demands of his angry comrades. He could have said, "You're right. The mistake I made is unforgivable. Let someone else take over." Many people in his position would have sunk into a deep, self-loathing depression. "But David found strength in the LORD his God." And in that strength he followed a well-conceived plan, tracked down the Amalekites, and rescued everyone and everything. "David got back everything the Amalekites had taken, and he rescued his two wives. Nothing was missing: small or great, son or daughter, nor anything else that had been taken" (vv. 18, 19).

Friend, I doubt that you're ever going to face a situation as guilt-inducing as the one David faced that awful day. But if you ever do, the same God who strengthened and equipped David for what he needed to do will strengthen and equip you as well.

I want to close this chapter by sharing something in the Bible that most people overlook, especially those of us who struggle with guilt and inferiority. It's the amazing number of times the Bible makes reference to innocent people. I'm guessing you'll be surprised to learn that (by my count) the word *innocent* shows up 119 times in twenty-eight different books. Here are some examples:

- "Day by day the LORD takes care of the innocent, and they will receive an inheritance that lasts forever" (Psalm 37:18).
- "The guilty walk a crooked path; the innocent travel a straight road" (Proverbs 21:8).
- "By smooth talk and glowing words they deceive innocent people" (Romans 16:18).

Clearly, it's possible to be a sinner and still be innocent at the same time. It's possible to be weak, needy, mistake prone, and guilty of a million sins and still be considered innocent—not guilty—by God.

How is this possible? Only through the blood of Jesus.

First John 1:7 says, "The blood of Jesus, his Son, cleanses us from all sin." Hebrews 10:22 says, "Our guilty consciences have been sprinkled with Christ's blood to make us clean." And Romans 5:9 says, "We have been made right in God's sight by the blood of Christ."

Notice that phrase "in God's sight."

If you are in Christ, God doesn't see ugly, filthy stains when he looks at you.

Satan certainly does. Others probably do. You very well could. But not God. In his sight you are pure, sparkling, and innocent.

That doesn't mean you don't still have some work to do. Paul tells us, "Work out your salvation with fear and trembling" (Philippians 2:12, *NIV*). In other words, apply yourself to the daily, sometimes difficult business of being a disciple. Guard your heart, clean up your language, use your talents to help build God's kingdom, and yes, get on that exercise bike once in a while. But while you're pedaling, don't worry about your status.

> **If you are in Christ, God doesn't see ugly, filthy stains when he looks at you.**

God says you're not guilty. It would be a tragedy for you to go through life believing and acting as if you are.

Don't let that happen.

HEADING FOR HOME

1. If you've been feeling guilty, take some time and think about why. Is there some sin—either an isolated incident or an ongoing situation—that you have not dealt with? If so, what's stopping you from repenting, apologizing, and making restitution? And if such a sin isn't present in your life, are you now ready to admit that your guilt is unjustified?

2. Of the four methods Satan uses to trigger accusations against you—comparison, catastrophe, confusion, and criticism—which are you most susceptible to? What specific measures will you take to keep Satan's poisonous thoughts out of your head?

3. Moses outlasted his critics by staying the course and remaining faithful. What is your most common response to criticism? Check all that apply.

   - You return fire.
   - You get depressed.
   - You quit in a huff.
   - You go off on a guilt trip.

   If you have a harsh critic in your life right now, what are some specific ways you might be able to overcome that evil with good?

4. The Bible says that David found strength in the Lord when he was in a pit of guilt, but it doesn't say how he did it. What are some things you would do in order to draw strength from the Lord?

JESUS LOVES ME, THIS I HOPE

Underestimate the love of the crucified and risen Jesus, and the shadow of shame, guilt, and fear darkens our space without respite.

—*Brennan Manning*

Nothing in Scripture is easier to prove than the amazing love our Lord has for weak, imperfect people. More verses state this truth and more stories illustrate it than I could even begin to squeeze into these pages. As far greater scholars than me have pointed out, the Bible is one big love story from start to finish. And yet, there are times in our lives when no truth is harder to believe.

Picture Judas fashioning the noose that he will, in moments, sling over the tree limb and slip around his neck. He's not doing it because he's *forgotten* what Jesus said about his love and willingness to forgive. He's doing it because he can't bring himself to *believe* what Jesus said about his love and willingness to forgive.

Judas would have been there when Jesus said, "I tell you the truth, all sin and blasphemy can be forgiven" (Mark 3:28). That very statement may have been reverberating in the corridors of his mind as he was preparing the rope. But from somewhere deep inside him, another voice drowned it out: "Not *your* sin. Maybe others' sins can be forgiven, but not yours. You've gone too far."

Many of us come to this darkest of places sooner or later. We sin so deeply, or so stupidly, or so inexcusably, or so often that we assume a holy God has to be disgusted with us.

Not long ago I was talking to a distraught man who was in this place, and he told me that he wept one night when he heard his young son singing, "Jesus loves me, this I know . . ." He said, "Mark, I remember singing that song with such conviction when I was his age, but at this point, with all the mistakes I've made, the best I could do would be to sing, 'Jesus loves me, this I *hope*.'"

Do you know that feeling?

Are you in that dark place right now?

If so, let's look for a way out together. I believe we'll find it by thinking about three images of Jesus most often seen in Scripture.

> "With all the mistakes I've made, the best I could do would be to sing, 'Jesus loves me, this I *hope*.'"

SCARY JESUS

A number of years ago, I met a brand-new Christian, a man who was, to put it delicately, not very polished. His rough edges and colorful language tended to make seasoned Christians nervous. Yet he appeared to be very sincere in his faith and was taking a real interest in the Bible. One day we were talking about the Scriptures, and I said, "What's the biggest thing you've learned from the Bible so far?"

I will never forget his answer.

He said, "I've learned that Jesus is one scary dude."

I would never have thought of saying it quite that way, but instantly I knew what he was talking about. There is a sense in which Jesus can indeed be a little scary.

Ken Gire, one of my favorite authors, stumbled onto this reality when he was just a boy, as I suspect many of us did:

> The picture of [Jesus] that I remember most was an eight-by-ten-inch portrait framed on a wall in our home. His skin was smooth and tan. His hair silken and brown. His posture stately. His features airbrushed to perfection. His head was turned slightly to one side, eyes looking away, almost as if he had been posed by a photographer who told him not to look at the camera.
>
> As a kid who got into my share of mischief, snitching cookies

from the cupboard or sneaking loose change from my mother's purse, I was glad his eyes looked away.

I remember one picture, though, where his eyes didn't look away. While on vacation in California, our family visited a chapel where a picture of Jesus was the main attraction. We filed reverently into the wooden pews of the small room, and as the lights dimmed, we watched the arched doors in front of us slowly open, revealing a huge portrait of Christ.

What was remarkable about the portrait were the eyes.

Wherever you sat, the eyes looked at you. Not only at you but through you. Or so it seemed to me as a young boy with plenty inside I didn't want him seeing. And if that weren't spooky enough, if you stood up and walked around the room, the eyes followed you. I never knew how they did it. I still don't. But I still remember those eyes following me with their unblinking scrutiny.[1]

When I first read Ken's words, I had to smile. I too can remember being creeped out by a lot of the portraits of Jesus I saw during my childhood. But as I got older, it wasn't the portraits that scared me; it was some of the things Jesus said. Here are some examples:

- "If you are even angry with someone, you are subject to judgment!" (Matthew 5:22).

- "Anyone who even looks at a woman with lust has already committed adultery with her in his heart" (Matthew 5:28).

- "So if your eye—even your good eye—causes you to lust, gouge it out and throw it away" (Matthew 5:29).

- "Do not resist an evil person! If someone slaps you on the right cheek, offer the other cheek also" (Matthew 5:39).

- "On judgment day many will say to me, 'Lord! Lord! We prophesied in your name and cast out demons in your name and performed many miracles in your name.' But I will reply, 'I never knew you'" (Matthew 7:22, 23).

- "Don't imagine that I came to bring peace to the earth! I came not to bring peace, but a sword. 'I have come to set a man against his father, a daughter against her mother, and a daughter-in-law against her mother-in-law'" (Matthew 10:34, 35).

- "For many are called, but few are chosen" (Matthew 22:14).

- "Give to anyone who asks; and when things are taken away from you, don't try to get them back" (Luke 6:30).

- "Anyone who puts a hand to the plow and then looks back is not fit for the Kingdom of God" (Luke 9:62).

- "It is easier for a camel to go through the eye of a needle than for a rich person to enter the Kingdom of God!" (Luke 18:25).

I doubt there's a serious Christian alive who hasn't swallowed hard when reading those verses and many others like them. Writing about Jesus' Sermon on the Mount, where many of those unsettling quotes are found, Philip Yancey said, "I . . . ask myself how to respond. Does Jesus really expect me to give to every panhandler who crosses my path? Shall I abandon all insistence on consumer rights? Cancel my insurance policies and trust God for the future? Discard my television to avoid temptations to lust? How can I possibly translate such ethical ideals into my everyday life?"[2]

Millions of believers struggle with these questions, especially new Christians who were under the impression that our Lord said only warm, fuzzy stuff. I couldn't begin to count the number of times over the last three decades that I've sat down with troubled people to discuss some hard saying of Jesus that was worrying them half to death.

But not just the pictures of him and the things Jesus said make him scary. Some of the things he did make him scary too.

Remember the time he cleared the merchants out of the temple? (Matthew 21:12, 13). Jesus took them to task for two reasons. First, they were price gouging. They were charging poor out of towners unreasonable fees for the money-changing services they needed in order to purchase unblemished animals to offer as sacrifices. Second, and perhaps most important, they had dragged their filching operation into the temple. A place that was supposed to be dedicated to prayer had become a den of thieves.

Certainly we can understand Jesus being upset. The surprise comes when he doesn't first seek a peaceful resolution to the problem. Didn't your momma teach you to try talking things out first, to avoid a physical confrontation if at all possible? Well, it looks like Jesus might have been daydreaming when that speech was given. He apparently just stormed in and started overturning tables. I can imagine people scurrying to get out of the way as bulging coffers tumbled onto the ground, frightened animals squawked in panic, and feathers flew.

If you want an even scarier example, think about the time Jesus cursed a fig tree. In the world rankings of obnoxious entities, I don't imagine trees rank very high. Seriously, if you were going to make a list of all the things in this world that deserve to be cursed, how long would it take you to get to a tree? Yet the Bible tells us that Jesus was hungry one day as he was passing by a fig tree. He walked over to it, planning to pluck a few figs, and discovered that there weren't any. So he cursed that tree with enough curse energy to make it wither instantly. Even the disciples, who were watching the whole thing, were stunned (Matthew 21:18-20).

Now please understand; I am not criticizing anything Jesus said or did. He was always right in every choice he made, and he always had good reasons for saying the things he said and doing the things he did. But some of his words and actions (not to mention those creepy portraits) can seem pretty scary if they're all you're looking at, especially if you've got some serious guilt and inferiority issues working. You could easily convince yourself that Scary Jesus is impossible to please, that someone with such high standards could never be happy with a buffoon like you . . . which is why you need to see another image of Jesus in the Gospels.

> You could easily convince yourself that Scary Jesus is impossible to please, that someone with such high standards could never be happy with a buffoon like you.

SYMPATHETIC JESUS

In complete contrast to Scary Jesus is the Jesus of kindness, compassion, and understanding—Sympathetic Jesus. Throughout the Gospels we see him in places he easily could have avoided, reaching out to those he easily could have judged, and offering help and encouragement he easily could have withheld.

For centuries people have been trying to disconnect Jesus from the real world, to perch him high on a pedestal, to make of him a stained glass image, regal and pious with arms outstretched, gazing down on the miserable wretches at his feet. But nothing could be further removed from reality. Bruce Marchiano says it beautifully: "We see Jesus in the streets day after day, offering people His kingdom in exchange for their pain. We see Jesus feeding the hungry masses, reaching His carpenter-calloused hands into the filth of a leper's sores, washing people's feet, starving in the wilderness, lifting cripples out of the sand, pulling prostitutes into His embrace. We see dirt and fatigue, struggle and striving. We see a man on a mission like no man has ever been on a mission before or since."[3]

When Jesus said, "Healthy people don't need a doctor—sick people do" (Matthew 9:12), he was defining that mission. The reason he's often called the Great Physician but never the Great Theologian is that even though he spoke theologically rich words, the thing that endeared him to people was his willingness to step into their messy lives and make a difference.

Speaking of theology (the study of God), I love the story about the disheveled man sitting in a hotel room talking to his pastor on the phone. The man's wife had just kicked him out, his sixteen-year-old daughter was pregnant, his seventeen-year-old son was in jail, his house was in foreclosure, his business was failing, and he'd just learned that he might have cancer. So he said to his pastor, "Please, you've got to help me. I just have to know . . . is Revelation 20 literal or figurative?"

> **The thing that endeared him to people was his willingness to step into their messy lives and make a difference.**

It's the absurdity that makes us smile. Theology is a wonderful thing, but we know that's not what messed-up people are looking for. We're looking for help and hope, which is what Sympathetic Jesus offered when he said, "Come to me, all of you who are weary and carry heavy burdens, and I will give you rest" (Matthew 11:28).

There are numerous peripheral characters in the Gospels who encountered Sympathetic Jesus, but one of the most intriguing is the woman caught in adultery (John 8:1-11). She was thrust before Jesus by an arrogant, smirking band of religious big shots. The fact that she was caught in the act sets our minds spinning. Somehow, it smells like a setup. Women in that mind-bendingly conservative, stone-throwing culture had plenty of incentive to keep their sexual indiscretions a secret, yet somehow she was caught in the act. Just how *did* her captors know what was going on at that precise moment behind that closed door and those pulled curtains?

I've often wondered how much remorse the woman felt—possibly very little. Perhaps the stolen embrace she was ripped from was the closest thing to love she'd ever experienced. I have no doubt that the hands of her illicit lover were gentler than those of the pompous Pharisees who saw her only as a pawn to be manipulated in their plan to embarrass Jesus. Maybe this is part of the reason why our Lord was so tender toward her.

But she couldn't have known that he would be.

In fact, it's possible that she knew him only as Scary Jesus. Perhaps she'd heard rumors about his hard sayings. It wouldn't surprise me if her heart caught in her throat when the crowd parted and she suddenly realized that the rabbi who'd spoken so harshly against the sin of adultery was to be her judge. She must have thought she was doomed. She must have believed that everything was set up for her complete annihilation, that the house of cards that had been her life was one flick of a finger from falling completely apart.

But it didn't happen.

After confounding the Pharisees and sending them off muttering to themselves, Jesus turned to the woman. I somehow picture all of Heaven holding its breath as the perfect God and the pathetic sinner stood face-to-face. Talk about gripping drama! If ever there was a perfect spot in the script of eternity to insert a lecture or a scolding or a scathing rebuke, this was it.

Instead, Jesus initiated the briefest but most telling of conversations:

"Where are your accusers? Didn't even one of them condemn you?"

"No, Lord," the woman responded.

"Neither do I. Go and sin no more."

At the very moment when this woman could have lost everything, Jesus *gave* her everything. Surely she looked at him in astonishment. Perhaps she even pinched herself to make sure she wasn't dreaming. I have no way of knowing, but I suspect it was the tenderness in his eyes and most definitely the hint of a smile that told her this was not a cruel joke.

In his book *Moments with the Savior*, Ken Gire imagines this woman years later with a husband and children, still tearing up from time to time at the thought of how things might have turned out if Jesus hadn't stood between her and the bloodthirsty Pharisees who were already hefting the rocks with which they planned to kill her.[4]

So we can see in the Gospels both Scary Jesus and Sympathetic Jesus, the condemner of sins and the forgiver of sins, the overturner of tables and the overturner of sentences.

If you find this a bit confusing, you aren't the first. Many a beleaguered believer has short-circuited his brain trying to understand why Jesus would curse a fig tree but forgive an adulteress.

Here's what I'm sure of:

We who struggle with guilt and inferiority tend to see Scary Jesus first. We might not see Sympathetic Jesus at all, or if we do we look away quickly, believing ourselves unworthy of such kindness. At best, we ping-pong our eyes between the two, wondering whether to feel doomed or hopeful.

What we need is something to break the tie . . . something to convince us that divine love truly exists for messed-up people like us.

And that's exactly what the Bible provides.

SUFFERING JESUS

Today on my lunch hour I was driving through Kissimmee and heard an astonishing news report. A man in Chicago was on his way to his local blood bank to donate blood for the four-hundredth time! As one who feels about needles the way I do about boa constrictors, I shuddered. As one who doesn't even like those finger-prick blood tests, I can't even imagine giving enough blood to float the *Queen Mary*. But I have to respect anybody who would. There's no telling how many lives that man has helped save.

Jesus gave blood too, only he didn't do it in a sterile room, stretched out in a recliner. He didn't have a cute little nurse administering the IV. He didn't get a free cup of orange juice and a cookie when he was done. And with Jesus there would be no coming back to give more blood in the future, because when he was finished there was no more left to give.

If you have even a shred of doubt about the Lord's love for you, take a look at Suffering Jesus. Picture him on the cross and think about how he got there. He wasn't drafted. They didn't draw straws in Heaven. He didn't make a couple of wrong turns and end up there by accident. On the contrary, Philippians 2:7, 8 says, "He gave up his divine privileges; he took the humble position of a slave and was born as a human being. When he appeared in human form, he humbled himself in obedience to God and died a criminal's death on a cross."

> **If you have even a shred of doubt about the Lord's love for you, take a look at Suffering Jesus.**

Notice, his divine privileges weren't taken away; he *gave them up*.

The humble position of a slave wasn't forced on him; he *took* it.

Then he obediently *humbled himself* even further.

In other words, nothing about Jesus' cross experience was forced, accidental, or inadvertent. It was his plan all along.

Not long ago, I heard a politician talking about our troops. He said there are no greater heroes than those who are willing to risk their lives for the welfare of others. Such a sentiment makes a nice political speech in wartime, but it just isn't true. The greater heroes are those who *give* their lives for the welfare of others. If you risk your life, you at least have a chance of surviving. But if you walk into a roaring buzz saw so that others might live, you've gone as far as a human being can go. Jesus himself said, "There is no greater love than to lay down one's life for one's friends" (John 15:13).

Then after he said it, he did it.

At the tender age of thirty-three.

As I write these words, I am fifty-three. Two decades ago I was the age Jesus was when he laid down his life. During the twenty years since, I have had most of the greatest experiences of my life. To think about what I would have missed if I'd died at thirty-three makes my heart ache. To think about what I would not have seen and heard and felt makes me unbelievably thankful that the Lord has graciously given me these years.

All of which makes me ask, Why didn't Jesus live longer?

If he'd been just a little cagey, surely he could have delayed the big showdown for a few years. Can you imagine the treasure trove of sermons and parables and miracles we would have to draw on if he'd lived his three score and ten? I mean, couldn't he still have gone to the cross at the age of sixty or seventy? It wouldn't have diminished his sacrifice, only delayed it long enough to expand his body of work and score more points for his kingdom.

But there's a reason why Jesus didn't live to see old age.

It's simply that he didn't come here to live—he came here to die.

Yes, he had to accomplish certain things before his death would mean anything. He had to fulfill prophecies, conquer every diabolical temptation his archenemy Satan could muster, and show us what God looks like with skin on. I'm not suggesting for a moment that his life had no purpose, only that his ultimate goal never was to establish an impressive résumé or to log a ministry career worthy of a retirement party and a gold watch. From day one, Jesus' all-consuming goal was to pay the price for our sins by shedding his blood. Consider these words from Isaiah: "He was oppressed and treated harshly, yet he never said a word. He was led as a lamb to the slaughter. And as a sheep is silent before the shearers, he did not open his mouth" (Isaiah 53:7).

Why didn't he open his mouth? Why didn't he make a plea for leniency and try to cop a little more time to spread his message? For that matter, why

There's a reason why Jesus didn't live to see old age. It's simply that he didn't come here to live—he came here to die.

didn't he call down legions of angels and have them go Jack Bauer on his executioners? Because he didn't come here to live—he came here to die. As he said himself, he came to give his life "as a ransom for many" (Matthew 20:28).

1 + 1 + 1 = 1

So there are three images of Jesus to be seen in Scripture. The problem is that two of them seem to fit nicely together, but one— Scary Jesus—just doesn't seem to belong. He is the proverbial fly in the ointment, the raspberry seed stuck between your tooth and gum. Think of the children's game (often on the back of a restaurant kiddie menu) in which the child is shown several objects and asked to identify which one is different. Scary Jesus seems different. He's like the neighborhood bully who shows up uninvited and crashes your party. You don't want him around, but you don't know how to get rid of him.

Try embracing him.

You see, Scary Jesus is one and the same person as Sympathetic Jesus and Suffering Jesus. In fact, all three of them combine to make Supreme Jesus, God's ultimate expression of love and a rather enigmatic mathematical equation: $1 + 1 + 1 = 1$.

Think about it.

Scary Jesus and his hard sayings, though they make us nervous and seem terribly oppressive at times, are necessary to keep the bar of righteousness raised high. Like a loving parent who sets up boundaries for his children—and chastens them when they ignore those boundaries—our Lord loves us too much to let us blindly follow our urges into Satan's clutches. And make no mistake, that is exactly where they would lead us. Instead, our Lord desires a far better life for us, found not at the end of the descending path of least resistance but on the mountaintop. So he pushes us to climb, to engage in a lifelong struggle for elevation, a lifelong battle against spiritual gravity, even though he knows it will be painful for us at times.

That's where Sympathetic Jesus comes in. We need to know that *our* pain is *his* pain. When the climbing gets hard . . . when Satan tries to knock us off the mountain . . . when blood-test results, divorce papers, a pink slip, or an eviction notice blows the world into a million pieces, we need to know that there's someone who cares . . . someone who will stoop down and help us pick them up and put them back together.

But in the end it would all be a waste of time without Suffering Jesus. All the moral guidelines and sympathy in the world would be of little help and comfort if we had no way to be forgiven.

If you're struggling with guilt and inferiority . . . if you've sunk to the place where you think a holy God couldn't possibly stomach someone with a rap sheet like yours, look again at Jesus. Not at some limited, partial, preconceived version of him but at the totality of his life and work. You will find that he is love. From every vantage point, in every situation, he is love.

There is a legend about John the apostle, who is often called the apostle of love and who referred to himself as "the disciple Jesus loved" (John 13:23). One day many years after Jesus had ascended to Heaven, John was going on and on about the amazing love of Jesus. One of his young disciples spoke up and said, "John, his love is all you ever talk about. Can't you talk about anything else?"

And John responded, "What else is there?"[5]

Let me close with a final word of encouragement: Please don't allow your emotions to overrule the truth of Scripture.

If the Bible says you are loved, then you are, whether you feel it or not. In fact, Satan will do everything in his power to make sure you *don't* feel it. What other option does he have? He knows he can't change the heart of God. He knows he can't change the truth of the Bible. So he opts for trying to change the way you think about it all. Don't let him succeed.

Remember, the song isn't "Jesus loves me, this I feel" and it's not "Jesus loves me, this I hope."

It's "Jesus loves me, this I *know*."

Go ahead. Sing it. At the top of your lungs.

You have God's promise that it's true.

And that's all you need.

HEADING FOR HOME

1. What was your impression of Jesus when you were a child? Did he seem scary to you, and if so, why? Has your image of him evolved as you've gotten older? In what ways?

2. Do you find any of Jesus' hard sayings particularly troubling? If so, what are some specific things you will do to try to make sense of them?

3. Many would say that we have to take a hard line against sin in order to keep it from proliferating. Why do you think Jesus allowed the woman caught in adultery to go free without so much as a reprimand? Have you ever been completely let off the hook in a situation where you were stone-cold guilty? If so, what impact did that show of grace have on you? Have you ever let a guilty individual off the hook that you could have easily punished? If so, why did you do it?

4. Circle the word in each of the following pairs of words that best describes your relationship with Jesus?

   - *Law* or *love*?
   - *Worry* or *peace*?
   - *Rules* or *relationship*?
   - *Effort* or *enjoyment*?

   Which of those words do you think Jesus *wants* to describe your relationship with him?

|||||||| **3** ||||||||

WHAT'S SO BAD ABOUT BEING GOOD?

Holiness hardly ever becomes a reality until we care more about Jesus than about holiness.

—Steve Brown

The writing of this book marks a turning point in my life. For the first time I am committed to giving up my relentless quest for perfection. For almost half a century, I denied that I was even on such a quest. When someone told me to lighten up and quit being a perfectionist, I politely explained that I was simply in hot pursuit of excellence, implying that the rest of the world (especially my accuser) was settling for mediocrity. Sometimes I even couched my response in spiritual terms, stating that God gave us his best and deserves nothing less from us in return. I especially liked that response because it made me sound so spiritual and no one dared argue with it.

But I now realize that my friends had me properly pegged all along. In fact, thinking back over some of my perfectionistic habits causes me to cringe at the absurdity of my denial.

For example, back in the days before personal computers and word processing programs, I would retype an entire 8½ x 11 page on my manual or electric typewriter rather than white out my typo with Liquid Paper and retype the single word I had messed up. To me that brush stroke of Liquid Paper was as ugly as a gash on a newborn baby's face. I needed my paper to have no blemishes whatsoever. (I wonder how many rain forests had to be cleared to provide all that paper I wasted.)

But I wouldn't admit to being a perfectionist.

When I was in Bible college, I was taught to preach from an outline fleshed out with a few notes, but that seemed far too imprecise for me. I needed to have every syllable I spoke predetermined and rehearsed to the hilt. So I started preparing word-for-word manuscripts and practicing them six or seven times before I had confidence to walk into the pulpit on Sunday morning. Even after all that preparation, I often lay in bed on Saturday night wondering if I needed to go over my sermon one more time just to be on the safe side.

But I wouldn't admit to being a perfectionist.

When I started doing interviews as an author, I tried to anticipate every conceivable question I might be asked. I sat for hours writing detailed, word-for-word responses and spent more hours practicing and memorizing those responses. I even had my wife do mock interviews with me. Yet after every interview I experienced disappointment and thought I should have done better. I would think back over questions I'd been asked and kick myself for not giving better answers.

But I wouldn't admit to being a perfectionist.

Trust me. I could go on and on with examples like this. What I've learned is that we can tell ourselves anything we want—and genuinely believe it—but that doesn't make it true. In spite of my denials, I was guilty as charged. I have indeed struggled with perfectionism my whole life. But starting today, I am picking up that proverbial new leaf and giving it a flip.

Why, you ask? What's so bad about being good?

A SERIOUS PAIN

For one thing, perfectionism is a serious pain. You don't realize this at first. You think you're pursuing something noble and good. You tell yourself that this quest is going to take you to wonderful places, to magnificent heights of accomplishment that few ever see or experience. You convince yourself that you're doing your part to make the world a better place. And then one day, sometimes after years and years of struggle, you realize that it's just a pain. A serious pain. In the patoot, as my grandmother used to say.

Pulitzer Prize–winning author Anna Quindlen came to this realization while still in school:

> I got up every day and tried to be perfect in every possible way. If there was a test to be taken, I had studied for it; if there was a paper to be written, it was done. I smiled at everyone in the hallways because it was important to be friendly, and I made fun of them behind their backs because it was important to be witty. And I edited the newspaper and cheered at pep rallies and emoted for the literary magazine and rode on the back of a convertible at the homecoming game and if anyone had ever stopped and asked me why I did those things—well, I'm not sure that I could have said why. But in hindsight I can say that I did them to be perfect, in every possible way. . . . And eventually being perfect became like carrying a backpack filled with bricks every single day. And oh, how I wanted to lay my burden down.[1]

I'm sure a nonperfectionist would read that and ask, "Then why *didn't* you lay it down? If your backpack full of bricks was so heavy and was making you so miserable, why didn't you just slip that puppy off your shoulders and chuck it? Why didn't you just stop being a perfectionist?"

Good question.

One answer is that while perfectionism is a pain, it also can produce some pretty nice results. The individual obviously never achieves perfection, but that doesn't mean he achieves nothing. Perfectionists are hard workers—some, even workaholics—and often very gifted. Therefore, it's not unusual to see them achieving more than their peers. Millions of perfectionists are sitting in high-paying jobs, living in big houses, and driving fancy cars. Let's face it. If perfectionism didn't pay off at least to some degree, no one would ever carry that backpack full of bricks. The fact that millions *are* lugging it around says something about the seductive power of this obsession.

> **Let's face it. If perfectionism didn't pay off at least to some degree, no one would ever carry that backpack full of bricks.**

Nevertheless, perfectionism is still a pain, for at least five joy-stealing reasons.

Reason #1: Perfectionism Is Never Satisfied

A salesman friend of mine said he always hated to set a new sales record for himself, because even though he got a nice commission check, his ungrateful, money-grubbing boss would then push his monthly quota higher and say, "See, I knew you weren't reaching your potential. I knew all along you could do better." That's perfectionism in a nutshell. It's never satisfied. Like an overbearing taskmaster it shrugs off your record-setting accomplishments and wants to know what you're going to do for an encore.

Reason #2: Perfectionism Keeps You Guessing

People define perfection in different ways, so as you move from one school to another, one job to another, one relationship to another, or even one church to another, you can be hit with a whole new set of expectations to try to live up to.

For example, I know an attractive, dark-haired woman who was married for a number of years and then got a divorce. A few months after her divorce was final, I ran into her and was stunned to see that she had become a blonde. Later her best friend told me that she was dating a man who preferred blondes. I shudder to think what other changes she made in order to become his perfect girlfriend. (I couldn't help speculating on what she might look like if she ever started dating a guy who preferred redheads.)

Reason #3: Perfectionism Takes Up All Your Time

I know a woman who spent all day shopping for the perfect pair of shoes to go with an outfit that she was planning to wear to an important social function. After spending an exhausting (and expensive) day on this quest, she ended up going back to the first store and buying the exact pair of shoes she had tried on seven hours earlier.

I can't say anything because I've done the same thing with my writing. I've spent hours, even days, rewriting a section of a book, only to end up chucking it all and going back to the original draft. You see, when you're a perfectionist, you waste enormous amounts of time trying to improve on things that are just fine the way they are. You just can't leave well enough alone.

Reason #4: Perfectionism Throws Your Life Off Balance

You can become so obsessed with the pursuit of perfection that you don't allow yourself time to just relax and enjoy life. The very idea of going golfing or fishing or even taking a nap seems like a frivolous waste of time when there's so much important work to do. The sad thing is that even after you've stripped all the fun out of your life and worked yourself half to death, you're *still* not satisfied. That's when the realization hits: you might as well have played that round of golf or gone on that fishing trip with the guys. But even then we perfectionists rarely learn. The next time we are faced with the same choice—take a break or keep grinding away—we repeat the mistake.

> We perfectionists rarely learn. The next time we are faced with the same choice—take a break or keep grinding away—we repeat the mistake.

Reason #5: Perfectionism Chips Away at Your Relationships

The nonperfectionists in your life eventually get tired of you always trying to impose your obsession on them.

A good example of this comes from my Little League coaching days. I always made my players tuck in their shirttails and wear their caps straight. One rather sloppy boy drove me crazy because his cap (along with just about every other article of clothing on his body) always seemed to be crooked. Finally, I created a hand signal that I could give him from the dugout to let him know he needed to straighten his cap. At the time I told myself I was helping him, instilling a little discipline, and teaching him to take some pride in his appearance. I now realize I was just imposing my obsession on him. Of course, he had to put up with it because he was a kid and I was his coach. If he'd been an adult, I suspect he would have told me what I could do with my cap rule.

No one knows for certain how a person becomes a perfectionist. Almost everyone agrees that the tendency starts at an early age. Some think it's inherited. Others believe it has a lot to do with the way we're treated when we're young. Still others theorize that sibling rivalry, giftedness, and even birth order are contributing factors. The only thing we can be sure of is that no parent who is a perfectionist would ever want his child to grow up and become one, because it's a serious pain.

But that's not the worst thing.

A SPIRITUAL PROBLEM

Most people write off perfectionism as just a harmless, although irritating, personality quirk. After all, you never flip on the evening news and see a person being loaded into a police car for being a perfectionist. You never see a newspaper headline that reads, "Perfectionist Apprehended After High-Speed Chase." On the contrary, perfectionists generally make valuable contributions to society and often are envied for their success. But make no mistake: this obsession flies in the face of some critical teachings of Scripture and can take you to a joyless place, far from God. Perfectionism is a spiritual problem.

Perfectionism Makes Contentment Impossible

Look at this stunning statement from Solomon: "A man might have a hundred children and live to be very old. But if he finds no satisfaction in life and doesn't even get a decent burial, it would have been better for him to be born dead" (Ecclesiastes 6:3).

If he finds no satisfaction in life . . .

This is your curse if you are a perfectionist. No matter how hard you try . . . no matter how many long hours you put in . . . no matter how good your projects turn out, you are never satisfied. You can't look at anything you do and call it good enough, whether it's building a shelf or being a parent. Every time you walk by the shelf, you stop and squint at it, thinking it might be a little crooked. And every time your child misbehaves, you think you are a complete failure.

That's a very dangerous way to live.

In his book *Jumping Hurdles*, Steve Brown tells about a twenty-six-year-old woman he knew who was on staff at a church. After college she had served for a year on the mission field. She was well liked, she maintained a strong witness, and she was an articulate spokesperson for evangelical Christianity.

But one day she killed herself.

Brown concluded that she had "created a false standard of perfection (or accepted someone else's standard)" and simply couldn't live up to it.[2]

We can imagine that the people around this young woman, including Steve Brown, didn't realize how hard she was grinding every day to try to achieve this standard. To them she looked like a model Christian, the kind of person who would be filled with joy, but inside she was experiencing more and more hopelessness. As her perceived failures piled up, her hope of ever achieving any semblance of contentment dwindled. Finally, like Solomon, she apparently came to the conclusion that if you can't find any satisfaction in life, you might as well be dead.

Of course it's true that not every perfectionist commits suicide. But this story points to one of the subtle dangers of perfectionism: you can eventually get so frustrated, so tired of not measuring up, that you quit trying. For this young woman, that meant suicide. For a greater number of people, it means abandoning family, faith, career, or whatever has them so frustrated.

I'll never forget a man I knew years ago who was walking out on his wife and kids. People assumed his departure was tied to lust. "Must be having a midlife crisis . . . must have a girlfriend tucked away somewhere," they said. But that wasn't the case. He simply considered himself a colossal failure as a husband and father and was running from the pain. I realized this when he said, "Mark, it's not like I'll be *more* of a failure if I leave."

I'll admit that when I was a young preacher, I didn't pay much attention to the Bible's commands and exhortations regarding contentment. Surely there were much more important things I needed to be talking about, much greater virtues I needed to be promoting, and much worse sins than discontentment I needed to be railing against. I don't believe this anymore. I now realize that Paul's statement in 1 Timothy 6:6 is foundational: "True godliness with contentment is itself great wealth." At the very least, contentment means the difference between joy and frustration. At the most it means the difference between keeping the faith and abandoning it. Either way, it's critical.

> At the very least, contentment means the difference between joy and frustration. At the most it means the difference between keeping the faith and abandoning it.

Perfectionism Focuses More on Doing Than Becoming

Proverbs 4:23 says, "Guard your heart above all else, for it determines the course of your life." With that statement God established that our primary focus should be on the development of the inner person, that our character is more important to him than our accomplishments. Most perfectionists can grasp this intellectually but have a terrible time making it real in everyday life because they are so hung up on performance, which is entirely external.

I know this all too well.

As a pastor I am judged on my Sunday morning "performance." (I hate to use that word with reference to the preaching of the gospel, but it's necessary to make the point.) I walk out onto a stage and do my thing in front of hundreds of worshipers who are, whether they realize it or not, judging me. I know full well that they will leave church thinking I was either good or lousy. They will have no idea what's going on in my heart, but they will either give glowing reports to their friends or tell them how boring I am, based on that twenty-five minute performance. On top of this, I know that our first-time guests will probably never come back if they aren't sufficiently impressed.

And then there's this writing gig. So many people assume that an author's life is glamorous. If glamorous means continually jumping through hoops to try to please people, then I guess it is. You have to write something an agent will like well enough to take you on as a client. Then you have to write something a publisher will like well enough to offer you a contract. Then you have to write something the book-buying public will like well enough to keep your book from bombing and putting you out of the business quicker than you got into it.

The point is that as a person who struggles with perfectionism, it's very easy for me to pour all my effort and energy into those performance-related things I do that stand to bring me the most approval. That confounded little voice down inside me keeps whispering that if the church grows, if my sermons get rave reviews, and if my books are all best sellers, I will be a success.

But is that true?

Not necessarily.

In 1 Samuel 16:7 God said, "The LORD doesn't see things the way you see them. People judge by outward appearance, but the LORD looks at the heart." Man looks at church-growth numbers and oratory skills and books sales, but God looks beyond all that.

In my case, I'm sure he's more interested in what I'm thinking about in my quiet moments, my attitude toward the person who wronged me, and whether I care enough to give a helping hand to a struggling brother. He's much more concerned about how I treat my wife than how clever my next book idea is. And he'd surely be curious to see if I'm as excited about talking to *him* as I am about taking a call from the talk-show host who wants to schedule an interview.

First Peter 3:3, 4 says, "Don't be concerned about the outward beauty of fancy hairstyles, expensive jewelry, or beautiful clothes. You should clothe yourselves instead with the beauty that comes from within, the unfading beauty of a gentle and quiet spirit, which is so precious to God." Granted, Peter was speaking to women, but the principle applies to everyone. Our primary focus should be on the inner person.

> **Man looks at church-growth numbers and oratory skills and books sales, but God looks beyond all that.**

Perfectionism Devalues People and Relationships

Not only do perfectionists tend to neglect the inner person, they also commonly neglect their loved ones. Not intentionally, of course. Nobody says, "OK, as a part of my overall life strategy, I've got to make sure I ignore my wife and kids." But it often works out that way as the perfectionist knocks himself out trying to achieve.

Jonathon Lazear wrote a book with a clever title, *The Man Who Mistook His Job for a Life*. In it he makes a confession that many perfectionist workaholics can relate to:

> One by one, most of my friends dropped out of sight. The daily phone calls became weekly, then monthly, then every few months; then we didn't even bother to call each other anymore. We'd send the holiday greeting cards and family newsletters, but there was no intimate contact. Forget about getting together; I was way too important and busy to do that. No movies, games, drinks, or dinner. I told myself, if I paused for a moment to dwell on it (which I rarely did), that my family was more important to me than my friends, and my time was limited, so I had to focus on the family. Of course, I wasn't doing that either; it was just another rationalization.[3]

Healthy relationships are a critical part of God's plan for us. God said that it isn't good for a man to be alone (Genesis 2:18). It isn't good for the man, and it isn't good for the people who need the man. Therefore, anything that pulls us away from our loved ones or builds walls between us and them is undermining God's master plan and will ultimately take us to a desolate, lonely place.

Anything that pulls us away from our loved ones or builds walls between us and them is undermining God's master plan.

Perfectionism Causes You to Live in Fear

The Bible teaches that the fear of the Lord is a good thing. Beyond that, however, fear should have no place in our lives. Romans 8:15 says, "You have not received a spirit that makes you fearful slaves." Yet that is exactly what many perfectionists are.

Miriam Elliott and Susan Meltsner speak to this problem with great insight in their book *The Perfectionist Predicament*:

> *Because your goals and standards are so high and reaching them is the most important and sometimes the only measure of your self-worth, if you are a perfectionist, you spend a great deal of time worrying about what will happen if you don't live up to those lofty expectations. You are constantly on the lookout for things that could go wrong, things that might stop you from being the best there is, and thus deal yet another blow to your already shaky self-image. You live in fear of failing or being rejected, abandoned, criticized, ridiculed, ignored, or subjected to some other horrifying fate.*[4]

Elliott and Meltsner use the term *catastrophize* to describe imagining worst-case scenarios.

I know exactly what they mean.

I've done it a thousand times.

I remember the first time I was scheduled to appear on a television show for an interview. Many talk shows are taped, which reduces the pressure tremendously. But this one was live and would be accessible to 75 percent of the world's population via satellite. In the days leading up to the interview, I tortured myself with visions of catastrophe. I saw myself stumbling onto the set, misquoting Scripture, misunderstanding a question and giving a ridiculous answer, forgetting my talking points, developing an enormous pimple on the end of my nose, and even sitting in front of the camera with my fly open. The interview ended up just fine, but for several days my intestines were tied in a knot no Boy Scout could have duplicated.

Clearly, this is not how God wants his people to live, but such nightmares are the curse of every perfectionist.

It should be pretty obvious that if you're never content, if you're ignoring your inner qualities, if you're neglecting your loved ones, and if you're living in constant fear, you're not going to be anywhere near the kind of person God wants you to be . . . and that you *need* to be in order to live a joy-filled life. That's why you must overcome this problem. To be honest, it probably won't be easy, especially if you're my age or older and have been a perfectionist your whole life. You might even need to seek the assistance of a qualified counselor.

But there *are* some things you can do for yourself. In particular, you can allow the Word of God to do its work in your heart. Hebrews 4:12 says, "The word of God is alive and powerful. It is sharper than the sharpest two-edged sword, cutting between soul and spirit, between joint and marrow. It exposes our innermost thoughts and desires." That's where perfectionism lives—deep in our innermost thoughts and desires. It's comforting to know that there is something that can reach that deep and have an impact.

Let me close this chapter with three Scriptures that have helped me and that I believe you'll find to be very liberating.

First, Ephesians 1:4: "Even before he made the world, God loved us and chose us in Christ to be holy and without fault in his eyes."

This is the verse that ought to have every perfectionist dancing in the streets. It says that if you're a Christian you can quit trying to be perfect, because you already are! Through Christ, we are "holy and without fault" in God's eyes. Maybe not in our own eyes or the eyes of our peers, but what are those opinions compared to God's? His is the one that really matters.

Second, Philippians 3:12-14: "I don't mean to say that I have already achieved these things or that I have already reached perfection. But I press on to possess that perfection for which Christ Jesus first possessed me. No, dear brothers and sisters, I have not achieved it, but I focus on this one thing: Forgetting the past and looking forward to what lies ahead, I press on to reach the end of the race and receive the heavenly prize for which God, through Christ Jesus, is calling us."

If I had to sum up those verses in a single statement, it would be this: the Christian life is about progress, not perfection. For that reason you should never measure the distance between you and perfection (which is what all perfectionists insist on doing). That distance is completely irrelevant. If you want to measure something, measure the distance between where you are today and where you were yesterday. If you made a little progress in the right direction, even if it was just an inch, celebrate!

Last, 2 Corinthians 4:7: "We now have this light shining in our hearts, but we ourselves are like fragile clay jars containing this great treasure. This makes it clear that our great power is from God, not from ourselves."

You might be thinking, *OK, this is all well and good, but my weaknesses still bug me.* Perhaps they won't bug you as much if you realize that God can use them to his glory. When people see a weak, imperfect person doing significant things for the kingdom, they will know, as this verse says, that God must be working, and they will glorify *him* rather than you.

> **If you want to measure something, measure the distance between where you are today and where you were yesterday.**

If you're a savvy Bible student, you probably noticed that all three of these passages were written by the apostle Paul. It's just my opinion, but based on these and other verses Paul wrote, I think he also must have struggled with perfectionist tendencies. I can't imagine it being a coincidence that he kept writing just the words we perfectionists need to hear.

Or shall I say, we *recovering* perfectionists.

Starting today, I'm heading in a new, happier, healthier direction. Won't you join me?

HEADING FOR HOME

1. Do you have any habits, quirks, or obsessions that indicate a struggle with perfectionism? Have you ever been accused of being a perfectionist? If so, what has been your typical response?

2. Everyone agrees that the pursuit of excellence is a good thing. In your opinion where does the pursuit of excellence end and perfectionism begin? If you know someone you believe is a perfectionist, what specific qualities lead you to this conclusion? Do you see any of those qualities in yourself?

3. Do you have any strained or withering relationships in your life? If so, is it because you haven't given them the time and attention they need? In general, when you are laying out your schedule, do you first consider people or projects?

4. Do you have a tendency to catastrophize (to imagine worst-case scenarios when you're faced with an important task)? If so, how many times has the worst happened? Where do you believe your worried thoughts are coming from? What will you do the next time you catch yourself catastrophizing?

IT'S OK, PART 1

Why do rules and regulations proliferate in a faith that promises freedom? Is freedom really that dangerous?

—*Tom Hovestol*

Jim Croce sang a song about certain things you just don't do if you know what's good for you. You don't tug on Superman's cape, spit into the wind, pull off the Lone Ranger's mask, or mess around with some dude named Jim. Let me add one more thing to the list. You don't let someone who struggles with inferiority translate the Bible. Never, under any circumstances, do you do this.

Why?

Because if you do, the Bible will be so big you'll need a crane to lift it and a truck with a HEMI to transport it from one place to another. People who battle inferiority have a knack for reading more than God wrote and hearing more than God said. Eve, who revealed her sense of inferiority when she so quickly and thoughtlessly grabbed what she thought was a chance to become something more than God made her to be, is a good example.

Way back at the beginning of time, God was very clear when he gave Adam instructions about the tree of the knowledge of good and evil: "You may freely eat the fruit of every tree in the garden—except the tree of the knowledge of good and evil. If you eat its fruit, you are sure to die" (Genesis 2:16, 17). However, just ten verses later, Eve is conversing with the serpent and says, "It's only the fruit from the tree in the middle of the garden that we are not allowed to eat. God said, 'You must not eat it or even touch it; if you do, you will die'" (Genesis 3:3).

Did you catch that?

Eve misquoted God!

"You must not eat it" became "You must not eat it *or even touch it.*"

Five words turned into nine. A simple command became a little more complicated. An easy command became a little more challenging. Something that wasn't a sin (touching the fruit) was granted sin status.

Given time, Adam and Eve probably would have built a wall around the tree, with barbed wire coiled along the top and maybe a couple of guard towers. They would have erected signs that said, "Beware! Do not touch, smell, look at, or even talk about the fruit on this tree. To do so is punishable by death!"

Yet all God said was, "Don't eat it."

Eve's story illustrates why we must never, ever allow a person who struggles with inferiority to translate the Scriptures. Every single one of God's commands will be expanded and made harder to keep. Things God never said will suddenly become the law. "Love your enemy" will become "Love your enemy and make sure you remember to send him a birthday card." I'm telling you, the Bible will be a foot thick! (A foot and a half if you're talking about the large print edition.) Inferiority places a lens in front of your eyes that makes everything—and I do mean *everything*—look like a sin. Consequently, you never feel good about yourself and never get to enjoy the assurance of your salvation. You mope when you walk and whine when you talk. You worry when you should have peace. Your life becomes one big guilt trip.

That's why I'm going to spend the next two chapters drilling two words into your head:

It's OK.

There are ten common activities that the inferiority crowd has granted sin status. My goal is to revoke that status . . . to show you why these

> **There are ten common activities that the inferiority crowd has granted sin status.**

things are *not* sins, why *it's OK* for you to do them, and why you're not going to Hell if you've *been* doing them. I offer them in no particular order, five in this chapter and five in the next.

It's OK to Make Your Own Decisions

She sat on our couch one evening with her face in her hands, weeping. No, her husband hadn't left her for another woman. No family member had died. She hadn't just been diagnosed with a terrible disease. Her distress stemmed from the fact that she desperately wanted to accept Christ and be baptized but she was afraid to. Her parents had raised her in a different religion and had threatened to disown her if she abandoned it. The pile of used tissues growing beside her on the cushion was a testimony to her agony.

Marilyn and I needed to be very careful as we talked with this young woman. We didn't want to say anything disparaging about her parents. On the other hand, we wanted to help her understand that there was nothing wrong with her as an adult making her own decisions, especially in a matter as personal as faith.

Notice I said "as an adult." Obviously, children should honor their parents. In no way am I advocating defiance of parental authority by ten- and eleven-year-olds. However, when you're in your late twenties, as this young woman was, it's OK to think independently of your parents and make your own decisions.

Then again, it's not only parents who can be controlling.

Peer groups can discourage you from thinking for yourself. Or you might have a domineering spouse who won't even let you breathe without getting permission. And then of course there are the cults, the undisputed world champions of mind and behavior control. There's no telling how many people in the world live every day with the paralyzing fear of doing something that might upset the controlling authority figure in their lives.

But it's OK to think for yourself and make your own decisions! Proverbs 13:16 says, "Wise people think before they act." What would be the point of thinking if you're always going to do what someone else tells you? Romans 14:12 says, "Each of us will give a personal account to God." Note the word *personal*. It means that all those people who love to control you are going to be nowhere in sight when you stand before God. They're not going to be there to explain how *your* mistakes are all *their* fault. So why should you blindly follow everything they tell you to do, especially when your gut (not to mention the Word) tells you they're wrong?

Something else to consider would be the many examples of independent thinking we find in Scripture. Caleb and Joshua disagreed with their peer group when reporting on the land of Canaan (Numbers 14:1-10). David rejected the counsel of his commander in chief before he marched out and shut Goliath up once and for all (1 Samuel 17:38-40). Paul ignored his best friends when they begged him not to go to Jerusalem (Acts 21:10-13). And do not overlook the fact that all of these men were risking their lives. The expedient thing would have been to conform to the wishes of others. Clearly, part of their greatness is found in their unwillingness to violate their consciences.

> All those people who love to control you are going to be nowhere in sight when you stand before God.

And here's something else to think about. Most of the threats made to try to hem you in ultimately come to nothing. Once someone sees that his hold on you has been broken, he will generally adjust to accommodate your new position. He might have a few choice words to share. She might play the martyr for a while. But when they see that your mind is made up, generally they will accept your decision. In most cases, controlling people know they're holding you with a paper chain; they're just hoping you never figure it out. When you do, your controllers typically shrug and make the necessary realignment. Case in point: the young woman I mentioned earlier in this chapter was not disowned by her parents. In fact, on the day she was baptized, they were there to see it!

If you've been living under somebody's thumb, you could probably dump a load of guilt and reclaim some self-respect simply by taking control of your life. Go ahead and do what you believe is right. It's OK.

It's OK Not to Try to Please Everybody

The key word here is *try*. We all know that nobody can please everybody, but that doesn't stop millions of us from trying. I did for years. Especially in the early days of my ministry, I believed a big part of my job was to make the people in the church I served like me. After all, how effective could I be if they didn't?

You wouldn't believe the hoops I jumped through. No matter what I was asked to do, I always said yes. On numerous occasions I sacrificed precious time with my family to attend concerts, recitals, ball games, banquets, and school programs that had nothing whatsoever to do with me, all because someone in the church invited me and I thought saying yes might win me some favor. Sometimes, even as I said yes, I was making a mental note to have my head examined.

All during this time I would have told you that trying to please everybody is a futile endeavor. I even preached it from the pulpit! But then I turned right around and tried to do it. Not until years later did I muster up the gumption to start saying no.

The first time was when I was invited to attend a Boy Scout banquet for no other reason than to say the prayer before the meal. I wasn't involved in scouting, didn't have a family member in scouting, and had no interest in scouting; but a lady in our church who was in charge of the festivities asked me to attend and make sure the fried chicken and mashed potatoes were properly blessed. I would be giving up an entire evening with my family to sit through an event I had no interest in, just so I could utter a thirty-second prayer before a meal that wouldn't be half as good as the one my wife would cook if I stayed home! For the first time in my life, I said no. I was nice about it, but I was also firm.

I'd like to tell you that the experience was liberating, but it wasn't. I experienced guilt feelings for days. In fact, the lady who asked me made sure I did. "Don't you care about the youth of our community?" she asked. She talked about what a great opportunity it would be to meet people, many of whom might be looking for a church. But guilt and all, I remained steadfast. Now, years later, I've become much better at saying no, but it was a hard wall to break through.

Here's what I always try to remember when I'm tempted to start jumping through hoops to make others happy: Jesus wasn't a hoop jumper. He did what he did and left it up to people to take him or leave him. In fact, John 6:66 says, "At this point many of his disciples turned away and deserted him." I'm sure Jesus was sad to see them go, but there's no indication that he tried to talk them into staying. There's no hint that he offered to change his ministry or preaching style to accommodate their opinions. Jesus wasn't a hoop jumper. His attitude seemed to be, "You're entitled to your opinion, but I have to be true to who I am."

> If you're pleasing God, you will also please most reasonable people. But if you're pleasing people, you can be a long, long way from pleasing God.

How much happier would you be if you could finally let go of your people-pleasing tendencies? More to the point, how much more joy would you experience if you spent as much time trying to please God as you do trying to please others? I've come to understand that if you're pleasing God, you will also please most reasonable people. But if you're pleasing people, you can be a long, long way from pleasing God.

It's OK not to jump through other people's hoops.

It's OK Not to Like Everybody

Will Rogers supposedly said, "I never met a man I didn't like." He obviously never met some of the people I've known! Like the guy who found fault with everything I did—and I *do* mean *everything*. Once I preached a sermon series on the life of Samson, a topic I knew pretty well because I had spent a year writing a book on the subject. This fellow stopped by my office and lectured me for not being a Christ-centered preacher. He said, "You're preaching on Samson when it's Jesus people need to hear about. *He's* the one who died for our sins, not Samson." Then he called me mercenary and said that I just preached to sell books and not to win souls. I can't think of a worse thing to say about a preacher. Preaching only for personal gain is the ultimate hypocrisy.

Week after week when I stepped into the pulpit to preach, that man sat with his arms folded across his chest and a sour look on his face. I admit it. I don't like that guy.

And for a long time, I felt guilty about it. I remember one day in a small group discussion when one very nice lady said, "Everybody has some good in them. Even a serial killer would help a little old lady across the street. So if you're a Christian, you're supposed to look for the good in others. You're supposed to give them the benefit of the doubt and be mature enough not to let their bad qualities affect your attitude."

That sounds so spiritual, which is why I walked out of that meeting feeling like a piece of dirt. Apparently I was not mature enough to be unaffected when someone looked me in the eye and leveled a terrible and unjust accusation against me. I couldn't just walk away reciting a list of my critic's good points.

Let me tell you where I found peace on this subject—in the story of Saul and David.

You may remember that Saul, the first king of Israel, was very fond of David at first. After David shocked the world by killing Goliath, he found himself on the fast track to fame. Saul promoted him to a position of leadership in the army, and David turned out to be a great leader. He and his men gave those old Philistines thunder. So much so that when they were returning from battle one day, the people chanted, "Saul has killed his thousands, and David his ten thousands!" (1 Samuel 18:7).

From that point on, Saul was jealous of David, and that jealousy quickly turned to hatred as David continued to become more popular. Eventually, Saul's hatred burned so hot that he made it his mission in life to kill David, forcing him to live as a fugitive, hiding out in the wilderness.

I noticed throughout this story that David was never under any illusions about Saul. In fact, he called Saul "evil" and "guilty" (1 Samuel 24:12-15). It's obvious that he didn't trust a word Saul said (1 Samuel 26:25–27:1). Clearly, he didn't like Saul. Not one little bit.

But he didn't mistreat him or try to get even. Even when he had opportunities to take Saul's life, David held back. On one occasion he said to his right-hand man, "Don't kill him. For who can remain innocent after attacking the LORD's anointed one?" (1 Samuel 26:9).

My conclusion: it's OK not to like someone as long as you don't harbor any ill will toward him, as long as you don't strike back when he hurts you, as long as you don't stoop to his level, and as long as you can find enough compassion in your heart to do him a good deed (Romans 12:19-21). David did Saul a *very* good deed when he didn't drive a spear through his head while he was sleeping (1 Samuel 26:5-9).

Jesus told us to love our enemies (Matthew 5:44). He didn't say we had to *like* them. If you can treat your enemies the way David treated his, your actions will fall well within the parameters of Jesus' command.

> **If you can treat your enemies the way David treated his, your actions will fall well within the parameters of Jesus' command.**

It's OK to Express Your Anger

Have you ever done anything in a fit of anger that you regretted?

When I was young, I had a hot temper. As a high school student, I was playing golf with my brother one day, when I hit a bad shot. I hauled off and threw my 7-iron about fifty yards down the fairway. I turned that thing into a helicopter. My brother, Mr. Self-Control, was disgusted, as well he should have been. When we got home, he told our parents that he couldn't stand to play with me because I acted like such an idiot. That was the last I saw of my golf clubs for several weeks. My parents confiscated them and told me that if I didn't get my anger under control, I would be in trouble my whole life.

That was a turning point for me. I started working on that weakness in myself, and today I can honestly say I have my temper in check. So much so that I now have the opposite problem—now I feel guilty when I get even slightly riled up! Sometimes I worry myself half to death over something I said, wondering if it was too harsh. On several occasions I have called someone to apologize when I wasn't even sure I'd said anything wrong.

Somewhere between comatose and a kicking, screaming fit is

a happy medium where anger is real but has no sin attached to it. Three passages of Scripture have helped me find that place.

The first is James 1:19, 20: "You must all be quick to listen, slow to speak, and slow to get angry. Human anger does not produce the righteousness God desires." The issue here is volatility. James doesn't say anger is wrong, only that you shouldn't have an itchy trigger finger. When something happens, your first response shouldn't be to blow somebody away.

A second helpful verse is Proverbs 19:11: "Sensible people control their temper; they earn respect by overlooking wrongs." This is called choosing the hill you want to die on. Some wrongs are not worth getting upset about and simply need to be overlooked. While irritating as all get-out, they are minor in the grand scheme of things. You know you've reached maturity when you can take a big-picture view of an incident, recognize its lack of importance, and find the grace to let it slide.

The third reference is Ephesians 4:26, 27: "'Don't sin by letting anger control you.' Don't let the sun go down while you are still angry, for anger gives a foothold to the devil." Grudges and vendettas are the by-products of anger that is allowed to fester. That's why it's so important to let go of your anger *the same day*. I've heard people say, "I'll get over it eventually," meaning that they intend to nurse their anger for a few days at least. But Paul's instructions are clear: "Don't let the sun go down while you are still angry."

Put all this together and you come up with some good boundaries for your anger. If you don't have a quick trigger; if you manage to control yourself, even to the point of letting some things slide; and if you don't let your anger fester and grow, it's OK to express it. Remember, Jesus rattled a few cages in his time.

It's OK to Change Your Mind

When I was in the eighth grade, I went out for track. I hated running, which is pretty much what track is all about, but a couple of my best buddies talked me into it. They convinced me that getting out in the fresh air and horsing around with them would beat sitting in study hall. This seemed reasonable because I loved horsing around and hated studying. And besides, they pointed out, I could sign up to compete just in a short sprint like the hundred-yard dash. Piece of cake.

But on the first day of practice, the first thing our coach did was send us off on a two-mile run around the perimeter of the school property. Not just the long-distance runners, but everyone. Suddenly, my short sprint turned into what seemed like a journey to the ends of the earth. I thought I was going to die. I wanted to strangle my now ex best friends.

That night I went home and announced to my dad that I had changed my mind about track and was retiring from the sport. He said, "Oh no you're not," and then he sat me down and gave me the "no son of mine is going to be a quitter" speech. It was a good speech. So good, in fact, that for years I felt guilty every time I got the urge to back out of a commitment that wasn't going the way I expected.

But eventually I developed a "theology of changing my mind" that has greatly helped me.

It starts in Ecclesiastes 3, where Solomon wrote that there is a time for everything. In verse 5 he says there is "a time to embrace and a time to turn away." We always assume that those two times will be far removed from each other, but why couldn't they come within hours or days? Isn't it reasonable to assume that there will be times when, with the best of intentions, we bite off more than we can chew? What kind of sense does it make to muddle onward when you know you just made a big mistake?

> Eventually I developed a "theology of changing my mind" that has greatly helped me.

From there I found my way to 2 Corinthians 4:8-10. Paul said, "We are pressed on every side by troubles, but we are not crushed. We are perplexed, but not driven to despair. We are hunted down, but never abandoned by God. We get knocked down, but we are not destroyed. Through suffering, our bodies continue to share in the death of Jesus so that the life of Jesus may also be seen in our bodies."

Putting those two Scriptures together, here's what I concluded:

First, I must never quickly or cavalierly walk away from anything important. When the going is rough and people actively oppose me, I must remember that it's during times of difficulty that a great witness for Christ can be put forth. And difficult times can be conduits of joy. The apostle James wrote, "When troubles come your way, consider it an opportunity for great joy" (James 1:2).

Second, not everything noble I commit to is going to work out the way I expect. Sometimes others won't keep their end of the bargain. Sometimes I will have made the commitment on faulty or incomplete information. Sometimes I just won't be as adept at it as I thought I would be. When that happens, it's OK to say, "On second thought, I'm not going to do this." In fact, it's more than OK; it's wise. Don't spin your wheels in futility for years, doing a lousy job, wasting resources, and burning yourself out simply because you can't admit you made a poor choice.

Are you starting to feel better yet? Take a break and answer a few questions, and then I'll continue on with more good news in chapter 5.

HEADING FOR HOME

1. Do you constantly worry about what's OK and not OK? Are there things you're doing that you feel guilty about, even though other Christians do the same things without feeling guilty? If so, where do you think your guilt comes from?

2. Is there a person in your life (or maybe more than one) who tries to manipulate you with guilt? How do you normally respond when such attempts are made? What will you need to do to change the dynamic of that relationship?

3. When evaluating right and wrong, are you more apt to consult the Bible or the opinions of your friends? Do you have enough backbone to make your own decisions about what's right and wrong, or do you normally bend to the thoughts and opinions of others?

||||||| **5** |||||||

IT'S OK, PART 2

*Blessed are those who don't feel guilty for doing something
they have decided is right.*

—*the apostle Paul (Romans 14:22)*

—————————╫—————————

In the last chapter I started revoking the sin status of some
common behaviors that make millions of people feel guilty. It's time
we realized that they are harmless and in some cases even healthy.
Here are five more.

IT'S **OK** TO QUESTION GOD

Some people believe that one of the hallmarks of strong faith is the
ability to accept everything that happens without questioning God.
Apparently, David didn't get that memo. The guy who dropped Goliath
with a sling and a stone while still a kid is famous for the strength of
his faith, yet he often questioned God. Here's one of many examples:
"O LORD, why do you stand so far away? Why do you hide when I am
in trouble? The wicked arrogantly hunt down the poor. Let them be
caught in the evil they plan for others. For they brag about their evil
desires; they praise the greedy and curse the LORD" (Psalm 10:1-3).

God is certainly not under obligation to answer every question we
fire at him. Proverbs 25:2 says that it's his privilege to conceal things.
But never does he tell us not to ask.

If you have children, you know exactly how this works. You never
mind when your kids ask you a question. Depending on their maturity

level or their need to know, you may or may not give a complete answer. But you always want your kids to come to you when they're troubled or confused.

One word of caution, however. There is a fine line between questioning God and criticizing him. Job is a good example of a guy who stepped over that line. You can read his story in the Bible book that bears his name. Basically, because of extreme suffering, he had a lot of pointed questions for God. They are sprinkled throughout the book. But at some point Job's questions morphed into sour complaints, prompting God to say, "Do you still want to argue with the Almighty? You are God's critic, but do you have the answers?" (Job 40:2).

Job wisely responded, "I will cover my mouth with my hand. I have said too much already. I have nothing more to say" (vv. 4, 5).

Yes, it's OK to question God. Just be careful. Don't forget who you're talking to. Be respectful. You just might get some answers.

It's OK Not to Be at Church Every Time the Doors Are Open

When I was a young preacher, I believed that in order to be a good Christian you had to have faith, confess Christ, repent of your sin, be baptized, and attend Wednesday night Bible study. The first four of those steps I could back up with Scripture. The last, not at all. But that didn't stop me from believing it. I am ashamed to admit it now, but for years I operated on the assumption that Christians who didn't show up at church every time the doors were open were somehow lacking in spirituality.

No doubt my attitude sprang from my upbringing. I don't remember a time growing up when there was a church service going on and our family wasn't there. Part of my frustration was the fact that *Walt Disney's Wonderful World of Color* was broadcast on television at six thirty every Sunday evening. All week long I saw commercials advertising that show, and it always looked so good, with adventures about pioneer explorers and pirates and wild animals. I would have given anything to stay home and watch. But no, we had to go to church. Why? Because that's what good Christians do. No, my parents never actually said that, but what else was I to conclude since we never, ever missed?

When I was nine or ten, I accidently spilled a cup of piping hot coffee on my leg. My skin blistered something awful and gave me my first real experience with excruciating pain. But there was an upside: because I couldn't wear pants, I got to stay home from church and watch *Walt Disney*! I'll never forget my emotions: I *loved* watching the show, but at the same time I felt like I was doing something illicit. Is it any wonder I entered the ministry ten years later with the notion that *real* Christians go to church every time the doors are open?

Thankfully, I have long since abandoned that notion.

First, I began noticing that the members of our church who attended every service were not necessarily our best members. Some of them were, of course. But others were critical and gossipy, and some were uninvolved. Even though they were present every time the doors were open, they weren't contributing anything ministry-wise and were, in some cases, causing trouble. That fact alone blew a gaping hole in my belief that the *best* Christians would always be the Wednesday night crowd.

Second, it eventually dawned on me that there is no biblical mandate for a Wednesday evening service—nor can you find Vacation Bible School, church camp, or even Sunday school in the Bible. Acts 20:7 says that our first-century brothers and sisters met "on the first day of the week" to share in the Lord's Supper. And yes, we're told not to neglect meeting together (Hebrews 10:25). But to turn those simple statements into a club for beating Christians over the head for not attending every single service or activity began to seem grossly unfair.

Finally, the across-the-board deterioration of the family that I was observing made me stop and wonder if the church was contributing to the problem. We asked people to make room in their already jam-packed schedules for a never-ending parade of church services and activities, and then we made them feel guilty if they chose not to. I started noticing that some of our people were dragging themselves to midweek services completely exhausted, a few even without dinner because they had come straight from work. Although grateful for their commitment and attendance, I eventually began to wonder if they were doing it because they wanted to or because they would feel guilty if they didn't. Further, I wondered if families would be better off staying home, enjoying some time together, and getting some rest.

Ultimately, I came to the following conclusions:

We are to worship God (Psalm 29:2) in spirit and in truth (John 4:24), on the first day of the week (Acts 20:7; 1 Corinthians 16:2). Beyond that, a host of church services and activities will be made available, but individual Christians must decide which of those are accessible and helpful. It's not my place (or yours) to pass judgment. Paul said, "So let's stop condemning each other. Decide instead to live in such a way that you will not cause another believer to stumble and fall" (Romans 14:13).

Honest. It's OK not to be at church every time the doors are open.

It's OK to Change Churches

A few years ago I wrote a book titled *The 10 Dumbest Things Christians Do* (Thomas Nelson). Dumb Move #5 was "Hopping from Church to Church." I will go to my grave believing that perpetually unsatisfied Christians who constantly bounce from place to place looking for the perfect church are more of a headache than a help to the kingdom. Great churches that impact their communities are not built by fickle church hoppers; they're built by dedicated Christians willing to hunker down for the long haul and do the hard and sometimes messy work of ministry. Chronic church hoppers are notoriously critical and undependable. Most preachers will tell you that they're more trouble than they're worth.

So here's what happened.

When that book landed on bookstore shelves, the e-mails started rolling in from people desperately dissatisfied with their churches but sure that switching would be something akin to a mortal sin. For the most part, they were conscientious Christians who did not want to church hop but believed they needed a change. E-mail after e-mail asked me pretty much the same question: Would it be wrong for us to leave a church we've been part of for so many years?

I could tell these poor people were being eaten up by guilt, so I compiled a list of reasons that I believe would make it OK to change churches. I'm not asking you to agree with this list, only to use it as a starting point for your own reasoning if you happen to be unhappy in your church.

When Doctrinal Purity Ceases to Be a Priority

If doctrinal purity has stopped being a priority at your church, I believe it's OK (and even advisable) to change churches. That we live in the age of relativism is old news. For years now our culture has accepted the notion that the truth is whatever best serves our purposes. Sadly, we're seeing more and more churches shape the gospel to serve their purposes.

For example, I recently came across a congregation with a rather odd view of baptism. Their official stance on baptism is that they have no official stance on baptism. If you want your baby sprinkled, they'll do it. If you want yourself to be immersed, they'll do it. And if you don't think baptism is important and choose not to do it, that's cool too. They don't want the baptism issue to be divisive, so they just throw the door wide open and declare anything and everything acceptable.

Obviously, this is an effort to be inclusive, but when it comes to doctrine, we aren't called to be inclusive; we're called to be faithful to the Scriptures. Paul said, "Let God's curse fall on anyone, including us or even an angel from heaven, who preaches a different kind of Good News than the one we preached to you" (Galatians 1:8). If you realize that your church is preaching "a different kind of Good News" without any corrective response from the overseers, it would be wise for you to find another church.

> When it comes to doctrine, we aren't called to be inclusive; we're called to be faithful to the Scriptures.

When Accessibility Becomes a Problem

It's very common nowadays for churches to relocate. The church I minister to has relocated twice in its thirty-year history. And not only do churches relocate, families do too. It's not uncommon for people to suddenly find themselves living twenty or thirty miles from a church that was once right around the corner. Depending on your finances (gas money), work schedule, and level of involvement, that kind of distance may make it impossible for you to have the kind of church experience you need. If you can't make it to worship consistently, if you have to give up your ministry involvement, or if your kids have to drop out of the youth group, it's definitely time to look for a good church closer to home.

For the Benefit of the Kingdom

If, for example, there's a new church plant or even a small, struggling church nearby that needs help, and if you happen to possess the skills or resources that are needed, you could be a tremendous benefit to the kingdom if you switched churches. Of course, this assumes that you wouldn't be leaving your old church in the lurch. It's hard to see how the kingdom benefits if the solution to one problem creates a brand-new one.

But beware! I've known people who've used this reason as a justification for their church hopping. Every year or two when the itch to move on hits them, they suddenly find a church nearby that desperately needs their help. It's their way of spiritualizing their lack of commitment.

When Hurts Become Overwhelming

We don't like to talk about it, but people do get hurt in church. Most of the time we're able to put those hurts into perspective, pray our way through them, and go on. But sometimes they're so deep that it becomes impossible to heal without a change of scenery. If, for example, your husband had an affair with a woman in the church, I doubt that you'd want to keep bumping into her every Sunday, nor would you want your husband to. Even if you completely forgave them both and believed there was no chance of the affair being rekindled, the flashbacks you'd experience every time you saw her could become a hindrance to your healing and your worship.

The idealist might say that you should stay put, show some maturity, and rise above your hurts no matter how deep they are. However, Proverbs 26:20 says, "Fire goes out without wood." Getting away from the source of your pain is one way to remove the wood so that your smoldering resentments can eventually die out completely.

My point is simply that all church-membership changes are not created equal. Some clearly are ill motivated and wrong, while others are wise and potentially faith saving. Even Solomon acknowledged that there is "a time to embrace and a time to turn away" (Ecclesiastes 3:5). When the time to turn away comes, you don't need to feel guilty about it.

It's OK to Shake the Dust from Your Feet and Move On

In the previous chapter we looked at changing our minds after we've made a bad or unwise choice. But what about those times when there's nothing wrong with the choice we made? What about those times when we're worn out and frustrated by someone else's choice or have done all that we can do?

From childhood we're taught to keep going no matter what. Motivational speakers traipse around the country exhorting people to hang in there. Gift books quote snappy sayings about endurance and perseverance. Films document the lives of people who never gave up and reached lofty goals as a result. Super Bowl and World Series winners always talk in postgame interviews about how the team never gave up (as if all the other teams did). Is it any wonder millions feel guilty for even *wanting* to quit?

Well, here's a news flash: it's OK to quit.

Under certain circumstances.

One of the best things my dad did for me was teach me to fish. He also instilled in me a certain philosophy of fishing. To his way of thinking, anybody can fish, but you aren't a real fisherman unless you use artificial bait. Anybody can get a fish to bite on a worm, but can you get a fish to bite on a little chunk of steel with a feather on the end?

> **Here's a news flash: it's OK to quit. Under certain circumstances.**

So I am to this day an artificial-bait guy. My favorite lure has always been a little spinner called a Shyster. Because it has to be cranked fast to create the spinning action, fish can't nibble on it. They have to hit it aggressively as it's zipping by, which creates hard strikes and a whole lot of fun. But there is a problem with this type of lure: it has a tendency to get hung up on underwater debris. If you're cranking *any* lure through the water at a good clip and it suddenly catches on an underwater log, you're in trouble. The hooks will likely sink into the log and be almost impossible to dislodge. You can yank and pull all day long, but the wiser choice would be to cut your line and tie on a new lure.

Sometimes in life you need to cut your line.

When you're hopelessly hung up . . . when you've tried everything and nothing has worked . . . when you've come to the place where your time and energy are wasting away and it appears nothing is ever going to change, quitting is an alternative that should be considered.

I'm sure someone will read this and take exception to my use of the phrase "hopelessly hung up." Someone will certainly take me to task for having small faith. I'll be reminded that faith the size of a grain of mustard seed can move a mountain, that there's always hope as long as God is on his throne.

OK, fine. But I am not the only one who believes there is a time to quit.

Jesus does too.

In Matthew 10 we read that Jesus sent the twelve out to preach and minister to the sick. He told them to travel light, to be hospitable, and to move on when they weren't well received: "If any household or town refuses to welcome you or listen to your message, shake its dust from your feet as you leave" (Matthew 10:14).

Jesus obviously recognized that there is such a thing as futility. Even for us who believe faith can move mountains, there comes a point when we're wasting our time and energy. We can stand there and yank all day, but the wiser option would be to cut the line and go fish somewhere else.

If this sounds cold, consider the fact that while you're busy yanking on a lure that isn't budging, hungry fish are swimming by. While you're busy trying to make an unworkable situation workable, great opportunities are just waiting to be seized. And this speaks to the most compelling reason why you sometimes need to quit. It's not because you don't have faith that something good might happen *eventually*; it's because time is short and there's so much you could be accomplishing *now*. Why keep yanking on a stuck lure when you could be catching fish?

Winston Churchill once said, "Never give in, never give in, never; never; never; never—in nothing, great or small, large or petty—never give in except to convictions of honor and good sense."[1] Those last two words are the key. Sometimes good sense tells you that it's OK to shake the dust from your feet and move on.

And now for the disclaimer.

I realize that more than a few people will read this and wonder if I'm giving them permission to bail out on their unhappy marriages. No, I'm not. Because of its sacredness, marriage is in a category all its own. Far more effort needs to be put into marriage than any other human endeavor I can think of. A wide range of scenarios could make quitting school, a job, a church, a routine, a relationship, or even a ministry a wise option. The same cannot be said for marriage.

It's OK to Take a Nap

In their book *Overcoming Overload*, Steve and Mary Farrar begin a chapter like this:

IKNOWWHATYOURETHINKINGSOMEONE MADEATERRIBLEMISTAKEINTHISPARAGRAPHIT MUSTHAVEBEENTHEPRINTERORPERHAPSTHE PROOFREADERBUTWHOEVERITWASSOME ONEWASNTDOINGHISJOBHOWINTHEWORLD DIDTHISPARAGRAPHMAKEITINTOTHISBOOK[2]

If these letters were spaced and punctuated properly, they would be easy to read. But because they are all run together, they are a mess. Something similar happens when we don't build any spaces (rest periods) into our lives. Physically, emotionally, and spiritually, we begin to deteriorate. The joy of our salvation slips away. This is why God established the Sabbath. Exodus 20:8-11 says,

Remember to observe the Sabbath day by keeping it holy. You have six days each week for your ordinary work, but the seventh day is a Sabbath day of rest dedicated to the LORD your God. On that day no one in your household may do any work. This includes you, your sons and daughters, your male and female servants, your livestock, and any foreigners living among you. For in six days the LORD made the heavens, the earth, the sea, and everything in them; but on the seventh day he rested. That is why the LORD blessed the Sabbath day and set it apart as holy.

I am not a proponent of the kind of superstrict Sabbath observance that makes everything other than praise and worship a sin. I'm merely reminding you that it's always been God's intention for his people to get adequate rest. Even Jesus took time to get away from the crowds to decompress and pray (Matthew 14:23). But in our full-tilt culture, *rest* has almost become a dirty word.

Take napping, for example.

In many ancient civilizations as far back as 500 BC, naps were taken for granted. People worked, ate, drank, and napped. No big deal. Even today in many parts of the world, napping is common. But in America, if you're a napper, you'd better be a preschooler or an elderly person (or maybe a college student who's just pulled an all-nighter). Otherwise, you'll likely be thought of as lazy or unmotivated.

> **Even Jesus took time to get away from the crowds to decompress and pray.**

There have been a thousand days when I've been tempted to kick my shoes off, stretch out on the sofa in my office, and take a little nap. But only recently did I do it. It was the middle of the afternoon. I didn't tell my secretary to hold my calls; I just stretched out and relaxed. I told myself that I wouldn't nap for more than ten or fifteen minutes and then I'd be up and at 'em again.

I must have been tired, because I woke up forty minutes later when some motorcycles with loud pipes went past our building. When my eyes popped open, I glanced at my watch and saw what time it was. I jumped off that couch as if someone had run a cattle prod up through the cushion. And yes, you guessed it: I felt guilty the rest of the day because I didn't get some of the work done that I was intending to do.

And that's the problem.

Most of us have so much on our plates that we think we have to be working every spare minute. But do we? I can attest to the fact that my world didn't collapse because I left a couple of things undone that day. Yes, I stressed about it, but looking back I can see that it didn't make one speck of difference. I just did those things the following day, and absolutely nothing was adversely affected.

I hope you understand that this section is not about sleep so much as it is about the need we all have to take care of ourselves without feeling guilty. Napping is only one way to build some pauses into your life. You could also have a daily quiet time, soak in a hot bubble bath, go for a leisurely stroll, watch a movie, put your feet up and read a book, or plan a weekend getaway.

One last thing.

How much pressure could you get rid of if you streamlined your daily routine and cut out the busywork? Chinese writer and inventor Lin Yutang said, "Beside the noble art of getting things done, there is the noble art of leaving things undone. The wisdom of life consists in the elimination of nonessentials."[3] If you're like most people, you've got some nonessentials in your life that are crowding the essentials. A few simple adjustments could give you more room to breathe and relax.

Glamorous movie star Katharine Hepburn won four Academy Awards, but late in her life she disdained glamorous clothing and dressed only to be comfortable.[4] She was said to own twenty identical pairs of beige slacks, twenty identical white shirts, and twenty identical

> **How much pressure could you get rid of if you streamlined your daily routine and cut out the busywork?**

black sweaters. She wore the same outfit every day because, as she said, "Dressing up is a bore." She must have understood that it was OK for her to do this, regardless of what the fashion police might think.

This is precisely the attitude I've been promoting in these last two chapters. The fashion police, the relationship police, the food police, the parenting police, the environmental police, the religion police, and above all, the political correctness police will have you feeling guilty about everything if you let them. You won't be able to dry your hands without worrying about the trees that had to be harvested to make those paper towels.

This madness needs to stop.

Everything is *not* a sin.

I love these words of Solomon and leave them with you as I close this chapter: "Do everything you want to do; take it all in. But remember that you must give an account to God for everything you do" (Ecclesiastes 11:9).

1. Do you blindly accept everything that happens, or do you question God? Describe what you believe would be the right way and the wrong way to question him. Do you ever refrain from questioning God for fear of not getting an answer? If you didn't get an answer, how would that affect your faith?

2. How often do you go to church? Are there times when you could go but don't? If so, why don't you go? Do you think you could benefit from going more often? Do you think going more often might have a negative impact on your life? If so, what would that be?

3. When a situation looks to be futile, are you more apt to quit or to muddle on through? Can you name something specific you're involved in right now that you need to get out of? If so, why haven't you done it?

4. What's your joy quotient been lately? When was the last time you took a nap? Did you feel guilty? What are some simple things you will do to create some pauses in your life?

YOU'RE NOT AS BAD AS YOU THINK YOU ARE

*Someone with a healthy sense of self may be the best candidate
to exercise true humility. Why? He has nothing to prove.*
—Stephen Arterburn and Jack Felton

When you hear the words *true confessions*, what comes to your mind?
Do you picture a Mafia hit man with his face pixeled out and his voice
electronically altered, sharing the secrets of his craft? Do you think
of a sultry mistress spilling the lurid details of her affair with a high-
profile politician? Do you imagine a best-selling book that chronicles
the comeback of a disgraced celebrity?

Not me.

Not anymore.

I think about moms. Plain old everyday moms, who drive their
kids to soccer practice and make macaroni and cheese for dinner and
clip coupons to help out the family budget.

I made this shift in my thinking when I found a book called *True
Mom Confessions: Real Moms Get Real*. It's aptly named because it's
chock-full of confessions made by real moms, many of whom betray
a strong sense of guilt and inferiority. Here are some examples:

- When people notice the improvement in my son's behavior, I tell
  them it's because I cut the red dye and refined sugar out of his
  diet. Actually, it's because I started seeing a therapist and stopped
  yelling at him so much, but how do I explain that?

- The goldfish didn't die of "natural causes" like I told the kids. I forgot to feed them.

- It's been one of *those* days. I just ate a full pint of Häagen-Dazs, and when my three-year-old asked me what I was eating, I told her it was special medicine for mommies because I didn't want to share.

- I was folding laundry yesterday and came across a pair of panties that were mine. My loving son (age eight) said, "There is no way those are yours, Mom. You are too fat to fit into them." I haven't eaten since.

- Sometimes when I'm holding my beautiful baby in my arms and we're gazing lovingly at each other, I secretly wish that she would fall asleep so that I could check my e-mail.

- I lean over my babies' beds at night when they're asleep and whisper, "I promise I'll be a better mommy tomorrow." There are just too many days I wish I'd done better.[1]

I don't question that these moms feel guilty, but as I thumbed through the book I sensed that many of them were being too hard on themselves. I mean, seriously, forgetting to feed the family goldfish is unfortunate, but it's not going to land you on the FBI's Ten Most Wanted Fugitives list. And what mother doesn't wish her baby would fall asleep so she could get other things done?

The moms who made these confessions are probably all better than they think they are. In fact, I've learned that most people who struggle with perfectionism, guilt, and inferiority are better people than they think they are. Way better.

You probably are too.

Not that you're not a sinner like everybody else. Of course you are. You need a Savior; I need a Savior; we *all* need a Savior. That's not my point. My point is that those of us who struggle with guilt and inferiority often are so predisposed toward self-criticism that we fail to see *any* good in ourselves.

> **Those of us who struggle with guilt and inferiority often are so predisposed toward self-criticism that we fail to see *any* good in ourselves.**

LET IT GO

What I want to do in this chapter is challenge your assumptions about yourself. I want to suggest eight possible reasons why you may not be as bad as you think you are. I know your natural tendency will be to dismiss these reasons out of hand and keep right on feeling bad about yourself, but I'm asking you not to do that. For once in your life, ditch the assumptions and try to be objective. Trust me; it's OK. (You did read the last two chapters, right?) It's OK to cut yourself some slack. It's OK to *not* beat yourself up. It's OK to be fair when you look into the mirror. All I ask is that you take these possibilities seriously, think them through, and see if they take you to a healthier place.

POSSIBILITY #1: YOUR EXPECTATIONS ARE UNREALISTIC

Apart from his off-course issues . . . more so than any golfer I've ever watched, Tiger Woods expects a lot of himself as an athlete. He expects to win every golf tournament he enters. He expects to hit every fairway, knock down every flagstick, and sink every putt. When he doesn't, it burns him up. Like the Sunday I watched him blast out of a buried lie in a greenside bunker, an impossible shot that he managed to stop within six feet of the hole. The crowd went wild and the announcers practically fell out of the booth as they showered him with praise. But did Tiger crack a smile? Not on your life. He slammed his wedge to the ground and stomped onto the green like a man who'd just discovered his car had been stolen. I'm sure he realized what a great shot he had just hit, but he was still steamed about the shot that put him in the bunker in the first place.

The thing about Tiger Woods is that even though his expectations of himself on the golf course are off the charts, they're not terribly unrealistic. He is so unbelievably good at what he does that nothing—not even the most outlandish challenge—seems out of reach. If he needs to sink a double-breaking forty-footer to win, he expects to be able to do it because he's done so many other mind-boggling things before.

A lot of us, on the other hand, have Tiger Woods expectations but not Tiger Woods talent. We demand things of ourselves that we're not capable of delivering. Don't get me wrong; I think goals should be set high. In fact, if you never fail to meet one of your goals, you're probably not setting them high enough. But setting high goals and setting unrealistic goals are two different things. If your goals are unrealistic, you will *never* hit them, and you'll end up feeling much worse about yourself than you need to.

Several years ago I started reading a lot of church-growth and motivational books. Though it goes against my nature, I was trying to get into success thinking and goal setting and achievement

> Setting high goals and setting unrealistic goals are two different things.

because it seemed to me that those were the things that the most successful preachers with the growing churches were into. But the more I got into it, the more discouraged I became. I wasn't seeing the dynamic results of the guys writing the books. I believed that I had some ability and I knew I was trying hard, but it just wasn't happening for me the way I expected it to.

One day I sat down with a successful preacher whom I respect a great deal. He rocked my world when he told me that he only had one goal: to be faithful to the Lord every day. He had no goals regarding church growth or building projects or any of the other things I was obsessing over. He said that as far as he was concerned, every day that ended with him in a healthy relationship with God was a good day, period. And then he added, "If you're faithful to the Lord every day, he's going to bless you, and all that other stuff is going to take care of itself." (Which, of course, sounds suspiciously like Matthew 6:33.)

That was the day I made a major adjustment to my goals and expectations. I lowered them in the sense that I reduced both the number and the scope. I simply decided to try to be the best Christian I could be every single day. And what a difference it made! Almost instantly I became a happier person, and in time I even became more successful in the areas I had previously been concerned about.

Now would be a good time for you to think about the expectations you've placed on yourself. If they're unrealistic, you'll repeatedly fall short and end up feeling a lot worse about yourself than you should.

Right now I have a friend who's going through a painful divorce. He's a dedicated Christian who has served the Lord faithfully for many years. The lives he's touched in a positive way would be impossible to count. I dare say that all of his friends and relatives would judge him to be a good husband, certainly far better than most. Sadly, the only person whose opinion matters disagrees. His wife wants out.

As a result, my friend is beating himself up. He understands what a sacred institution marriage is. The very last thing he ever wanted was to become a divorce statistic. Now that he has, he says he feels like a piece of trash.

But his focus is too narrow. When he looks at himself in the mirror, all he sees is a man who couldn't keep his wife happy. It's as if those countless admirable accomplishments on his résumé don't even exist.

I don't mean to minimize the seriousness of divorce. (Anyone who knows me would testify that I would never do such a thing.) But at the same time, it should be acknowledged that a man is more than his marriage, just like he's more than his career or his education or his parenting skills.

In Scripture, David is the perfect example. Let's face it; he would never receive an ounce of respect from anyone if he were going to be judged solely on his marital record. As you may recall, God had made it abundantly clear that the king of Israel "must not take many wives for himself" (Deuteronomy 17:17). But David did. In fact, he was so far off track from God's will in this area that he actually stole another man's wife (Bathsheba) even though he already had an entire harem!

But we don't think of David as a miserable failure, because we understand that there was more to him than his marital misadventures. David the ladies' man was also David the patriot, David the leader, David the warrior, David the military strategist, David the poet, and so on. In other words, to be fair to David (or anyone else), you have to look at the whole picture. We would do anyone a huge disservice if we focused only on his sins.

Is this what you're doing to yourself?

Do you have an embarrassing failure on your résumé that you've never let go of? Maybe you've repented and sought God's forgiveness, but you still insist on dragging the rotting corpse of that bad decision around with you so that you inhale the stink of it every single day. I'm not suggesting that you forget what you did; you need to remember so you won't do it again. All I'm saying is that at some point you need to bury the corpse and move on with your life, realizing that while that failure may be a *part* of you, it certainly isn't *all* of you.

POSSIBILITY #3: THE SOIL YOU'RE PLANTED IN ISN'T VERY FERTILE

There are many things I like about living in Florida and a few I don't. One of the things I don't like is that you can't grow a decent tomato here. In southern Illinois where I grew up, the tomatoes are juicy and flavorful. Here the tomatoes are dry and tasteless. The difference, of course, is the soil. Southern Illinois has soil that's black and rich with nutrients. Here, it's reddish brown and sandy.

This means that if a Florida gardener and an Illinois gardener had a tomato-growing contest, it would be . . . well, no contest. The Florida gardener could knock himself out babying his tomato plant and the Illinois farmer could do nothing but stick it in the ground and forget about it; it wouldn't matter. The Illinois farmer would still win. You don't have to have a green thumb to grow a great tomato in Illinois, because it's all about the soil. Any old city slicker can do it.

In one sense, people are a lot like tomatoes: some are blessed to be planted in fertile soil and others are not. As a pastor, I know very well how this works. Some of us serve in small towns where there is zero population growth, while others serve in thriving areas where thousands of new residents move in every year. Some of us serve in economically disadvantaged areas where just getting a leaky roof fixed is a major challenge, while others serve in communities where every other car on the road is a Lexus or a BMW and the church coffers are always overflowing. And some of us wear all the hats and fight all the battles alone while others have gifted staff members with specialized

> In one sense, people are a lot like tomatoes: some are blessed to be planted in fertile soil and others are not.

training supporting them. Obviously, it would be grossly unfair for pastors who are planted in sandy soil to feel bad about themselves because they're not having the success of those pastors who are planted in more fertile soil . . . but a lot of them do.

And it's not just pastors.

I know a perky little woman who's married to a guy with the personality of a doorknob. He's a very good person (which is why she married him), but he's just not very exciting. Not surprisingly, his wife is frustrated out of her mind. She longs for an exciting, romantic relationship with her soul mate and beats herself up because she can't make it happen. She's tried everything from lingerie to play-off tickets, but so far nothing has caused a spike in Mr. Deadpan's pulse. What she needs to realize is that this isn't her fault. She just isn't planted in the right kind of soil to have a storybook romance.

I could go on and on with examples, but you see what I mean. The soil you're planted in is going to have a lot to do with what you're able to produce in life. It could be that what you are producing is truly exceptional when the disadvantages and hardships you're dealing with are factored into the equation.

POSSIBILITY #4: THE PEOPLE YOU DEPEND ON ARE LETTING YOU DOWN

As I'm writing these words, March Madness is in full swing. (For you non sports fans, that's the NCAA basketball tournament.) Talk about a tough job . . . what could be more trying than to be a college basketball or football coach? For one thing, the stakes are unusually high. Football and basketball produce millions of dollars for the institutions, which is why said institutions feel so much pressure to win and are quick to fire coaches who don't deliver the Ws. But even more difficult to take than the pressure to win is the fact that, as a coach, your success—and therefore your future and your reputation—is in the hands of a bunch of teenage boys. You can do a great job of teaching your players about life and about the game, but you can't babysit them. When they leave practice, they're on their own. If they decide not to study or go to class, or worse, to get into trouble, they will suffer for sure . . . but so will you.

It's a sad fact of life: sometimes the people you depend on for your success or your health or your happiness let you down. Your spouse might cheat, your children might defy you, your employees might steal from you, your employer might mismanage the business and cost you your job, or your investment company might go belly-up and cost you your retirement. We live in a world where it's possible to experience epic suffering without doing anything wrong.

> It's a sad fact of life: sometimes the people you depend on for your success or your health or your happiness let you down.

Think about Caleb and Joshua as they returned from their spy mission inside the land of Canaan. They pleaded with the Israelites to trust God and march forward into the promised land in spite of the giants that inhabited it: "They are only helpless prey to us! They have no protection, but the LORD is with us! Don't be afraid of them!" Joshua and Caleb cried (Numbers 14:9). But the Israelites refused to budge. And not only did they refuse, they even started talking about stoning Caleb and Joshua if that's what it took to get them to shut up. At that point, our boys had no choice but to shut their mouths and suffer right along with their faithless countrymen.

As they tromped off into the wilderness, I imagine Joshua and Caleb second-guessed themselves, wondering what they might have said or done differently. Perhaps they beat themselves up for not being more persistent, for not finding a way to persuade the people. But the truth is, they did nothing wrong. It was the Israelites' failure, not their own.

You might be in a similar situation. Perhaps the failure you're coping with and the suffering you're going through is not your fault. Maybe the people (or the person) you were depending on failed miserably. If so, give yourself a break. Just because you're picking up the pieces doesn't mean you're the one who broke the vase.

POSSIBILITY #5: YOU'RE STANDING IN THE SHADOW OF GREATNESS

Shortly after my first book came out, my publisher invited me and several other authors to attend a reception for some of the most outstanding Christian retailers in the country. I can't tell you how honored and excited I felt because I knew authors like Max Lucado, Ted Dekker, and John Maxwell would also be there representing the publisher. As one who admires writers the way some people admire movie stars, I expected this to be a thrilling experience.

But it wasn't.

In fact, I've rarely felt as out of place as I did that evening. Why? Because no one knew who I was. They all assumed I was one of the retailers! I kid you not. I stood there all by myself while crowds flocked around the other authors.

One guy carrying a glass of punch and a cookie did walk over to me and ask, "So where's your store?"

"I don't have a store," I said. "I'm actually one of the authors."

"Oh really? What did you write?"

When I told him I had written *The Samson Syndrome*, he said, "Never heard of it."

It's easy to feel invisible standing in the shadow of greatness, especially if we struggle with inferiority. Fortunately, I only had to do it for one hour. Maybe you have to do it every day at work. Maybe you're married to greatness. Or maybe you're one of those with the Roman numeral II after your name, causing everyone to look at you in the light of your famous father's accomplishments. If you're not careful, you can start feeling like a misfit, a disappointment, or worse, an imposter.

> It's easy to feel invisible standing in the shadow of greatness, especially if we struggle with inferiority.

The good news is that God doesn't compare you to others. He understands that your DNA is like no one else's. The fact that you are surrounded by or married to greatness has no bearing on God's expectations of you. That's why Paul said, "Each of us will give a personal account to God" (Romans 14:12). "A personal account" means you won't slide in on someone else's coattails, but it also means you won't be diminished by somebody else's greatness. I'll take that deal any day.

POSSIBILITY #6: YOU BELIEVE THAT ABILITIES HAVE A PECKING ORDER

Almost everywhere you go in this world, respect comes (or is withheld) according to what we do. In a hospital, for example, people practically bow and scrape to a doctor but hardly notice the woman pushing the janitorial cart. (In case you're wondering, this explains why you can buy your preschooler a toy stethoscope but not a play toilet brush.) Even in church it's the preachers, singers, and authors who get all the glory, while nursery workers and lawn mowers and toilet scrubbers work in total anonymity and are lucky if someone ever thanks them for what they do.

The Bible clearly teaches that abilities do not have a pecking order, that they are all important to the health and success of the church. Paul even said, "Some parts of the body that seem weakest and least important are actually the most necessary" (1 Corinthians 12:22). I happen to think God detests the way his people swoon over authors and musicians and TV preachers we don't even know but never utter a word of thanks to those in our own churches who serve humbly and tirelessly without complaint, week after week.

I know this all sounds very obvious, but you'd be surprised how many people don't feel good about themselves because of the work they do. Not long ago I met a newcomer to our church and asked him where he worked. "I just work at Walmart," he responded. His tone and that word *just* told me that he believes in the ridiculous notion that what he does indicates his worth.

Do you?

Are you embarrassed to say what you do for a living? Only if you do something illegal, immoral, or unethical is that OK. Otherwise, your work is just as valid as anyone else's. Paul said, "Whatever you do or say, do it as a representative of the Lord Jesus, giving thanks through him to God the Father" (Colossians 3:17).

POSSIBILITY #7: YOUR VALUES ARE INVERTED

A man who came to see me had a failing business on his hands and one doozy of a debt. Our conversation went something like this:

He: This is so humiliating.

Me: It's a situation you have to deal with, sure. But it doesn't define you, because you've done so many other things well.

He: This is going to tie my hands financially for years.

Me: Maybe so, but look what a great job you've done with your family. You have a wife who loves you and great kids.

He: You don't seem to understand. I've got a huge problem here.

Me: This is what I understand and what you need to think about before you go jump off a cliff. Your business is failing, but your family is succeeding. As I see it, you got the most important thing right. You need to be thankful for that. I'm guessing there are a lot of successful businessmen with damaged, dysfunctional families who would trade places with you in a heartbeat.

You see the man's mistake, don't you?

He had allowed his values to become inverted. Things of secondary importance had overtaken things of primary importance in his mind. Consequently, he had lost the true measure of himself. He was actually a man of considerable accomplishment, but he viewed himself as a failure.

Jesus told a story about a man whose values were equally inverted. We call him the rich fool because he measured himself by the size of his barns and his ability to eat, drink, and be merry. Jesus' comment on the man's upside-down view of life was succinct. He said, "Life is not measured by how much you own" (Luke 12:15).

To measure yourself properly, your values have to be right side up. If they aren't, you'll feel good about yourself when you should feel bad and bad when you should feel good. If you're not sure what your values should be, get into the Word. Start with the words of Jesus in the Gospels and go from there to the book of Proverbs. Whatever you do, don't rush. Go slow, think about what you're

> **If you're not sure what your values should be, get into the Word. Start with the words of Jesus in the Gospels and go from there to the book of Proverbs.**

reading, and pray yourself along. As your values get properly aligned, you just might feel a whole lot better about yourself.

POSSIBILITY #8: YOU'RE PREJUDGING THE FINAL RESULT

There is an old saying that has been repeated in churches for as long as I can remember. Whenever you find a mean little kid who is the terror of the Sunday school, somebody will invariably say, "He'll probably grow up to be a preacher." They mean it as a joke and people always laugh, but you'd be surprised how often it actually happens.

I can honestly say that the two meanest little boys I've ever known both grew up to be missionaries. One of them happened to be in my wife's Sunday school class when he was about six years old. Never a Sunday went by that Marilyn didn't come home with some wild story to tell about that little monster. She was convinced he had deep psychological problems. Out of all the kids in the church, we had him pegged as the most likely to end up in jail.

Imagine our surprise years later when I picked up a Christian periodical and ran across an article about a missionary with the same name. I looked at my wife and said, "No way. It can't be!" But we did some checking and it was. The little psychopath had actually grown up to become a man of God.

This is why we should never prejudge anything or anyone, including ourselves, yet that's exactly what millions of us do. Especially those of us who are parents.

Perhaps right now you have a teenager who makes you feel like the worst parent in the history of the world. You look at his jeans (big enough for three people), you stare at his hairstyle (looks like a nuke went off on top of his head), you meet his friends (did they just arrive from another planet?), and you hear his music (which would make a car crash sound like "Brahms Lullaby"), and suddenly you begin to understand why some animals eat their young. You ask yourself where you went wrong and wonder if you could be imprisoned for releasing such a person into society.

Whatever you do, don't prejudge what your child will become, and don't condemn yourself as a failed parent before the end of the story has been written. Lots of weird teenagers have grown up to become excellent adults. In fact, if you were to think back to your high school years, you'd probably be forced to admit that you caused your own parents a few sleepless nights. Child-rearing expert Dr. Kevin Leman wrote a book, the title of which is a much-needed reminder: *Adolescence Isn't Terminal: It Just Feels Like It.*

As you reflect on these possibilities, please remember that I am not trying to cultivate a spirit of arrogance in you. Paul said, "Don't think you are better than you really are" (Romans 12:3). That's a clear command, but so is Paul's very next comment: "Be honest in your evaluation of yourselves." *That's* my purpose in this chapter, to help you be honest in your evaluation of yourself. As a person who struggles with perfectionism, guilt, and inferiority, you will always be inclined to be too hard on yourself, which is just as wrong as thinking too highly of yourself.

You may feel like a total failure most of the time. And you may be. But chances are you're not any such thing. Chances are you're not nearly as bad as you think you are.

HEADING FOR HOME

1. How would you describe your expectations of yourself? Approximately what percentage of the time do you think that you meet or exceed your expectations? When you fail to meet them, how do you handle it? Check any that apply.

   - You lower your expectations.
   - You push yourself harder.
   - You just sit there and feel bad about yourself.

   What *should* you do?

2. How fertile is the soil you're planted in? Do you honestly feel that your potential is limited by where you live, where you work, or other factors? Do others agree? If so, what can be done to change that dynamic? Is a relocation out of the question? How about a job change? How far would you be willing to go to find some fertile soil?

3. Name your two or three greatest abilities. Are you happy to have them or would you gladly trade them in for a new set? Have you spent your life lamenting the fact that you aren't gifted to do something specific? What adjustment will you make in your thinking to overcome that attitude?

4. If you're a parent, to what extent do your kids shape your view of yourself? Think back to your own growing-up years and reflect on how you might have made *your* parents feel. What changes will you make in your parenting style that could give your kids a better chance to succeed in life?

7

FACING (AND FORGIVING) YOUR FIRING SQUAD

It really doesn't matter if the person who hurt you deserves to be forgiven. Forgiveness is a gift you give yourself. You have things to do and you want to move on.

—RealLivePreacher.com weblog

The movie *Valkyrie* ends with a gut-wrenching scene. Tom Cruise's character is convicted of masterminding a failed plot to assassinate Hitler; he is marched outside and made to stand in front of a firing squad. His courageous demeanor no doubt stems from the fact that he knew all along that his traitorous activities, if unsuccessful, would earn him such a fate. With his chin held high and defiance in his eyes, he screams, "Long live sacred Germany!" a second before a volley of bullets rips into his chest.

You may never know the terror of standing before a real firing squad, but unless you're a hermit living in a cave, you'll have plenty of critics lining up to take shots at you. It won't matter if you've done anything wrong or not. In our hair-trigger culture, if you just pause for an extra second before stepping on the gas at a green light, some jerk a few cars back will, with a blast from his horn, let everyone within earshot know what he thinks of your driving ability. Honking horns, dirty looks, raised middle fingers, cold shoulders, gossipy comments, condescending attitudes, sarcastic remarks, and outright condemnation are just some of the weapons people use to mow each other down.

My concern in this chapter is not for the average Joe who gets shot at now and then. Everybody has to duck or dodge a bullet of criticism occasionally. Instead, my concern is for the person who *lives* in front of a firing squad. I'm thinking specifically of the wife whose obnoxious husband constantly berates her, the husband whose loudmouth wife never stops nagging, the employee whose irritable boss is never satisfied, or the public figure whose work makes him a popular target for every malcontent in his constituency. It is the rare person who can live with constant criticism and not start to have serious inferiority issues.

I realized pretty quickly after I entered the ministry that I had to find a way to process criticism if I hoped to keep my sanity. As one who already struggled with inferiority, I knew that living under the constant barrage of criticism, which is a fact of life for all preachers, would destroy me at some point. It didn't happen overnight, but I eventually learned to face and forgive my firing squad. In this chapter I'm offering some thoughts that helped me and may help you too.

> **It is the rare person who can live with constant criticism and not start to have serious inferiority issues.**

FACING YOUR FIRING SQUAD

In many movie firing-squad scenes, the condemned man is offered a cigarette and a blindfold. Sometimes, if he's extra tough or defiant, he'll refuse the blindfold, but never the cigarette. Here are three simple reminders that will do you considerably more good than either a blindfold or a cigarette.

Reminder #1: Your Firing Squad Could Be Shooting Blanks

Quite often the criticism leveled against you won't have any substance. It will be so out there that your most appropriate response will be to laugh, shake your head, and let it go. Allow me to give a couple of personal examples.

Many years ago I served a church where the elders (my bosses) were, shall we say, a tad nitpicky. One year during my annual evaluation, they spent half an hour lecturing me about how I didn't stand at the right door after our Sunday morning services. Our auditorium had several entrances, and I generally stood at the same door every week to "shake the people out." But it wasn't the *right* door, according to these elders. They believed that a different door accommodated slightly more traffic and would, therefore, offer more potential hands to shake.

I didn't say it (because I had no desire to become instantly unemployed), but I remember thinking that the world was going to Hell in a handbasket while we were sitting there discussing how I could maybe manage to shake twenty-five more hands by standing in a different spot. When I got home that night and told my wife about the discussion, she said, "Can't you see what a compliment that is? If that's the biggest criticism they have of you, then you must be doing a lot of things right."

That was the night it first dawned on me that sometimes the firing squad is shooting blanks.

Another example is more recent.

At Poinciana Christian Church I always give an invitation to accept Christ at the end of my sermon on Sunday morning. One morning, after giving the invitation and with the worship team poised and ready to lead the congregation, I said, "We're going to sing this little song. Please come now if you have a decision to make for Christ." Then the music began.

That week I received a note from an anonymous critic. It accused me of cheapening that moment in our service by using the words *little song*. "It isn't a little song," my critic wrote. "It's a big, important song because people, at that moment, are weighing decisions for Christ." I guess the person would have preferred that I say, "We're going to sing this big, important song. Please come now if you have a decision to make for Christ."

See what I mean? Some criticisms are so ridiculous that the only appropriate response is to

> **Some criticisms are so ridiculous that the only appropriate response is to shake your head and roll your eyes.**

shake your head and roll your eyes. (By the way, don't tell anyone, but for the next four weeks I said "little song" on purpose just to let my anonymous critic know that the unsigned letter did no good.)

Quite often, the guns pointed at *you* will be firing blanks too.

Reminder #2: Your Firing Squad May Not See the Big Picture

Think about the soldiers who put Jesus to death on the cross. They had no grasp of the significance of that moment. To them Jesus was simply one more common criminal who deserved what he was getting. As strange as it may seem, crucifying him was just another day at the office for them. That's why Jesus prayed, "Father, forgive them, for they don't know what they are doing" (Luke 23:34).

Of course it's true that the nails still hurt, even though the soldiers didn't realize what they were doing. The crown of thorns and the sword still drew blood. And in the end Jesus was just as dead as he would have been if the soldiers *had* known what they were doing. But in Jesus' mind it made at least some difference that his killers were, in a manner of speaking, clueless.

I've found that makes a difference for me too.

On many occasions I've been able to soften the sting of criticism by reminding myself that the people firing at me do not understand the nature of my job. They don't understand that I live in a fishbowl. They don't realize how many hats I wear. They don't stop to think about how many different needs I must take into consideration when I make a decision. They don't see the long hours I put in. And most of all, they may not be biblically literate enough to know the scriptural mandates that drive my ministry. It's amazing how people who don't know what you do, have never done what you do, and couldn't do what you do if their lives depended on it feel free to criticize you.

> In Jesus' mind it made at least some difference that his killers were, in a manner of speaking, clueless.

You may have the same experience if you're a single mom. Another woman who's never been a single mom might pick you apart. Or if you're a CEO, some guy who's never made more than minimum wage might talk about you like you're an idiot. The world is full of know-it-alls. You can let them get under your skin, or you can shrug them off and pray along with Jesus, "Father, forgive them, for they don't know what they are doing."

Reminder #3: Not Every Shot Is Aimed at Your Vital Organs

Remember the old cowboy movies where the gunslinger fires a few shots into the dirt at a man's feet just to make him hop around? If he wanted to, he could put any one of those slugs through the man's heart, but he doesn't because he's on a power trip rather than a killing spree. He gets his jollies not from making people dead but just from making them dance.

I know this type of person all too well. I'll never forget the guy who dropped by my office every morning on his way to work. And I do mean *every* morning. He always walked in with a smile and a friendly hello, which I returned. I'm sure he thought we were bosom buddies, but I never felt comfortable around him. He had mastered the implied criticism, statements that implied some deficiency on my part.

For example, he might say, "I stopped at the hospital yesterday to check on Miss Della, and she said no one from the church had been by to see her." Meaning, of course, that *I* hadn't been by to see Miss Della. Implication: I wasn't doing a very good job of caring for our elderly members.

Here's another example: "I was surprised when I didn't see you at the Cooper girl's wedding last weekend." Implication: You should have been there.

People who say things like this are not shooting at your heart; they're shooting at your feet. They're not trying to kill you; they're just trying to make you dance. And I did dance. This man was a powerful figure in the congregation, and I believed I had to please him in order to be successful there. I tried to correct all the deficiencies his comments hinted at. And the more I hopped around in an effort to prove myself, the more rounds he squeezed off. Looking back, I'm convinced that he enjoyed the control he had over me. And I hated myself for letting him have it.

I'd like to tell you that I quickly realized what was happening and stopped dancing, but the truth is that I let that man control me for the duration of my ministry with that church.

I've since learned that the more I try to be what some people want me to be, the less I will be what God wants me to be and the less likely I will be to accomplish God's purposes in my life.

Further—and this is huge—I've learned that these critics are all bark and no bite. In other words, if you ignore them, nothing bad will happen. They'll control you if you let them, but if you refuse to dance they'll back off. This is because deep down inside they are usually decent people. Controlling, yes, but still decent. If they weren't, they'd be shooting at your heart instead of your feet

> **The more I try to be what some people want me to be, the less I will be what God wants me to be.**

from the beginning. You will find it extremely liberating to embrace the fact that while you may have to put up with them, you don't have to dance for them.

So think with me for a moment.

If you take the total number of criticisms that will be fired at you and subtract all that are not worthy of a response—that is, those that are completely bogus, ill-informed, and fired at your feet—all of a sudden you've got a manageable number. That means the real key to facing your firing squad is simply to keep things in perspective. See every criticism for what it truly is. If it's a blank, don't act like it's a bullet. If it was fired at your feet, don't react like it was fired at your heart.

As a person who struggles with inferiority, this is one of the biggest lessons I've learned: reality is my friend. Things are almost always better than I first think they are.

FORGIVING YOUR FIRING SQUAD

Dealing with the bullets is only half the battle. Equally important is how you frame your thinking toward the person (or persons) firing the shots.

The first impulse most of us have is to roll out the heavy artillery and fire back. The very idea of dropping a bunker buster into the middle of the shooter's camp gives most of us shivers of delight. But the apostle Paul, playing the role of party pooper, eliminated that as an option when he said, "We are human, but we don't wage war as humans do" (2 Corinthians 10:3). He also commanded us not to take revenge for ourselves when we are wronged (Romans 12:19). But it was Jesus who completely cramped our style when he came up with what is undoubtedly the most unpopular command in the entire Bible: "Love your enemies! Pray for those who persecute you!" (Matthew 5:44).

As a person who struggles with inferiority, you ought to thank God for these commands. Yes, I know they're the last thing you want to hear when someone is taking potshots at you. But without them you'd probably follow the impulses of your sinful nature and end up destroying what little self-worth you have left. If the bullets themselves didn't finish you off, the shame of hating someone probably would. So I encourage you to embrace forgiveness. Don't see it as a command to be followed but as an opportunity to be seized. It's just one more step toward recovering your joy on the road home from your guilt trip.

> **Embrace forgiveness. Don't see it as a command to be followed but as an opportunity to be seized.**

Here are five facts that should make forgiving your firing squad a little easier.

Fact #1: Forgiving Allows You to Speak Your Mind and Defend Yourself

Forgiveness does not, as we often assume, require us to put on a muzzle and silently endure whatever our critics want to say about us.

Take Paul for example. The same guy who said we must never take our own revenge didn't hesitate to speak up and defend himself when he was being unfairly criticized. When his enemies were questioning his qualifications as an apostle, he thought it was important to set the record straight, so he spent almost three full chapters detailing his credentials (2 Corinthians 10-13).

Jesus did the same thing when Jewish leaders blasphemed him by saying he was possessed by Satan (Mark 3:22). He could have kept quiet, but he didn't. He defended his ministry, showed the illogical nature of their criticism, and even gave them a stern warning regarding the danger of blasphemy (vv. 23-29).

No doubt someone will say, "But wait a minute! What about Jesus' command to turn the other cheek? Shouldn't Paul and Jesus have taken whatever their critics wanted to dish out without fighting back? And shouldn't we?"

First of all, I would dispute the notion that Paul and Jesus in the examples I just mentioned were fighting back. Rather, I believe they were simply setting the record straight. Some important truths were being obscured, and they felt the need to respond. If they'd wanted to fight back, they would have launched a counteroffensive and tried to sully their critics the way their critics were trying to sully them.

Second, there are indeed times when no response at all is the best response to criticism. As Steve Brown said, "Most of the time, you ought to ignore criticism. After all, your enemies will believe it before they hear it; your friends won't believe it after they hear it; and most folks will never hear it anyway."[1] Based on my years of experience working with people, I would say that at least 75 percent of all critical remarks should be completely ignored. They're either so trivial or so far removed from the truth that only a completely unreasonable person would believe them . . . and you're not going to change an unreasonable person's mind anyway! Thus, such criticisms are simply not worth the emotional investment. Let them go. Turn the other cheek.

However, on those occasions when the truth *does* need a helping hand, you can feel free to offer an appropriate response. Forgiveness does not require you to wear a muzzle.

Fact #2: Forgiving Sets You Free

People who hate their enemies and plot to get even think they're free, but they're not. They are, in fact, more imprisoned than some who live every day of their lives behind bars.

I think about this every time I hear someone talk about getting revenge. You don't "get" revenge. You get gas. You get groceries. You get a check-up. But you don't get revenge; it gets you.

How?

By trapping you in a vicious cycle.

You do a slow burn over what happened. You fantasize about what you'd like to do to even the score. You sift through your options, looking for the most devilish one that has a realistic chance of working. You lay out a plan. You look for an opportunity to carry it out. You unleash your plan when the moment seems right. Then you wait for a response. If you don't get one, you think you didn't do enough and start planning all over again. If you *do* get one, you think your enemy is back to being one up and start planning all over again. Either way, you start planning all over again, which is a clear indication that you're trapped. You think you're "getting" revenge, but you're only getting frustrated. The truth is that revenge is getting you.

The only way out of this prison is forgiveness. When you let the offense go, and I mean *really* let it go . . . when you empty your heart of all bitterness and give up your desire to keep score, the prison door pops open and you are free to go your way and get on with your life.

Fact #3: Forgiving Gives Your Witness Wings

Right now there are probably observers in your orbit watching for indications of your spiritual integrity. They may know you're a churchgoer. They may see that prolife bumper sticker on the back of your car or that cross hanging around your neck. But in this cynical, suspicious generation, those things don't count for much. What people want to see is how you react under fire. Thus, your willingness to forgive your firing squad could be the thing that convinces them to take you and your faith seriously.

Earlier in this chapter I mentioned the prayer Jesus offered up from the cross for the soldiers putting him to death, a prayer of compassion and forgiveness that made a profound impression on the Roman soldier

> **Your willingness to forgive your firing squad could be the thing that convinces them to take you and your faith seriously.**

overseeing the crucifixion. Luke 23:47 says he became convinced of Jesus' innocence and even worshiped God right then and there.

Irish pastor Jim McGuiggan tells the story of a corporal in the army who informed his hard-living buddies that he had accepted Christ. They assumed it was just a stage he was going through. They couldn't believe that such a wild and crazy guy would be able to make that kind of dramatic change and stick with it, so they began hassling him at every opportunity. They made fun of him, told dirty jokes in his presence, played tricks on him . . . anything to try to turn him back into the good old boy they once knew.

One Saturday evening, one of the corporal's buddies staggered into the barracks after a tiring, day-long march. When he saw the corporal kneeling by his bunk, praying, he picked up his boots and threw them at him as hard as he could. One hit the corporal in the shoulder and the other hit him in the head.

When the soldier woke up the next morning, he found his boots, shined and polished, sitting on the floor beside his bed. He was so impressed by the corporal's forgiving response to a boot in the head that he turned to the Lord.[2]

Nothing gives wings to a believer's witness like forgiveness. Beautiful words, large financial gifts, and even backbreaking service can all be rendered with impure motives, but it's hard to imagine how forgiveness could be. When you willingly and without coercion wipe clean the slate of the person who's been shooting at you . . . when you cheerfully accept mistreatment and make no effort to even the score, what worldly benefit could you possibly hope to gain? People who do this deserve to have their faith taken seriously.

Fact #4: Forgiving Opens the Door to New Possibilities

When you forgive someone, you have no guarantee of ever getting an apology. You can't even be sure that the person who shot at you won't fire again the first chance he gets. But at least you open the door to the possibility of peace, reconciliation, and friendship.

Think about it.

Throughout our lives we are driven by possibilities, not guarantees. The possibility of getting a better job sends you off to college. The possibility of greater happiness causes you to say yes to a marriage proposal. The possibility of a longer, healthier life motivates you to say no to the cheese fries. Life offers few guarantees; it's possibilities that drive us.

Why should it be any different in our interpersonal relationships? If forgiveness is what it takes to create good possibilities with someone you're currently at odds with, why not go for it? If those good possibilities are never realized, at least you haven't lost anything. But if any of them are, think what you will have gained!

> **Life offers few guarantees; it's possibilities that drive us.**

Fact #5: Forgiving Means You Can Be Forgiven

You can make a tearful profession of faith and be baptized a hundred times in crystal clear Rocky Mountain spring water, but if you refuse to forgive someone, you're not going to Heaven. Jesus left no doubt about this when he said, "If you forgive those who sin against you, your heavenly Father will forgive you. But if you refuse to forgive others, your Father will not forgive your sins" (Matthew 6:14, 15).

Grudge bearers everywhere should take notice: there is no wiggle room here. Jesus leaves no loopholes. If you refuse to forgive, you disqualify yourself from being forgiven. It's as simple as that. On several occasions I've shown these words to a believer who was boiling with anger and determined to get revenge. I ask the person to read them out loud, and then I pose the question: "Are you really willing to trade your salvation for this vendetta?"

I don't think we should be in the business of ranking sins, but I do think this business of grudge bearing doesn't get the attention it deserves. Christians can get all up in arms over any sin with a sexual dimension. We huff and puff with righteous indignation when the subject of child abuse or abortion comes up. All these are horrible, but where can you find a more hard-nosed statement than this one

Jesus made about the refusal to forgive? Clearly, God is in the grace business, and he demands that his children be in it too.

John Maxwell said, "The way that you treat others is your statement to the world of who you are."[3] He's right, but I would sharpen the statement even more and say it this way: the way you treat *your enemies* is your statement to the world of who you are. It's easy to treat your friends the right way, but the critics taking shots at you present a challenge.

If you return fire, you're telling the world you're just like them. If you forgive, you're proving that you're different.

And you can feel good about that.

HEADING FOR HOME

1. Do you live with a lot of criticism? If so, what percentage of it do you feel you deserve? What are some things you will do to lower that percentage?

2. Does someone in your life love to fire at your feet and make you dance? How long have you been allowing him or her to control you in this way? What's preventing you from refusing to dance and taking back control of your life?

3. If it's true that 75 percent of all criticisms should be ignored, how would you rate yourself when it comes to responding to criticism? Check all that apply.

   - You fire back more often than you should.
   - You fail to set the record straight when you should.
   - You find pleasure in returning fire. (What do you think this says about you?)

4. Are you pursuing a vendetta against someone right now? If so, have you thought about what you're forfeiting? Is the desire for revenge truly more important to you than God's forgiveness?

8

POISON IN THE PULPIT

We love a man that damns us, and we run after him again
to save us.

—*John Selden*

When I was in high school, I worked for a florist after school. I loved delivering orders, because I spent all my time driving (a big deal to a sixteen-year-old) and putting smiles on faces. The florist said that he figured at least 25 percent of his business came from men with guilty consciences. To this day when I see a guy on his way home from work buying a dozen roses for five bucks out of the back of somebody's pickup, I figure there's a good chance he's in trouble at home and is trying to make up with his wife.

If you're a woman, I'm sure you can tell when your husband is feeling guilty. Out of the blue you get flowers, a back rub, breakfast in bed, or a love note on the refrigerator. I once heard a woman say that she wished her husband would misbehave more often because he was never nicer than when he had a guilty conscience!

It works the other way too. Any time a guy walks in from a hard day's work to find his favorite meal sitting on the table and his wife in a slinky outfit, purring like a B-movie sex kitten, you can bet he's going to be wondering how much she added to the credit card balance that day or how badly the car is dented.

Bottom line: guilt affects the way we behave. This explains why the world is full of . . .

GUILTMONGERS

A *monger* is a dealer or a trader. You've heard of warmongers and hatemongers. A guiltmonger is simply a person who deals in guilt.

I hate to say it, but some of the most notorious guiltmongers the world has ever known have been preachers. Which makes some sense. A preacher's work is all about getting people to do things they don't ordinarily feel inclined to do—making radical changes to their lifestyles, giving away their hard-earned money, donating their precious free time.

And when you find something that motivates as well as guilt, you're strongly tempted to serve up heaping helpings.

Charles Haddon Spurgeon (1834–1892) was an English preacher and pastor of the famed Metropolitan Tabernacle in London for over three decades. In 1856 he founded a pastors college where he lectured extensively on the art of preaching. Those lectures are still available and make for some interesting reading. They indicate, for one thing, that Mr. Spurgeon was not the stuffy old codger his picture makes him out to be. Hilarious observations and ringing one-liners filled the lectures and indicate that he knew very well the ways of the guiltmonger and was determined to keep his students from going down that road.

Consider, for example, this rather acerbic passage: "Much the same may be said for the numerous hammer-men who are at work among us, who pound and smite at a great rate, to the ruining of Bibles and the dusting of pulpit cushions. . . . Their one and only action is to hammer, hammer, hammer, without sense or reason, whether the theme be pleasing or pathetic."[1]

Hammer-men. We call them pulpit pounders. They are the yellers, the screamers, the slingers of fire and brimstone. The guiltmongers.

Granted, this type of preacher is not particularly in vogue right now. They're not writing the best-selling books and being interviewed on the morning news shows when a catastrophe happens, because

> And when you find something that motivates as well as guilt, you're strongly tempted to serve up heaping helpings.

our generation has embraced a kinder, gentler style of preaching that often makes a sermon seem more like a chat with Mr. Rogers. But make no mistake; the hammer-men are still out there in thousands of churches all across the country, karate chopping pulpits left and right.

I know of a church that has just such a preacher. I haven't heard him, but I can assume he's a hammer-man (and wants to be known as one) because the sign in front of his church building announces to passersby that the church uses *only* the *King James Version* of the Bible. How's that for laying down the law before someone even steps through the door? Where did they come up with the idea that just one version of the Bible is truly of God? I think they found it in that storehouse where all narrow and judgmental ideas are found, and that it wasn't the only one they plucked off the shelf.

Recently a man and his wife from out of town arrived at our church about forty-five minutes before our first service, while our worship team was rehearsing. I immediately put down my sax, walked to the back of the auditorium, and greeted them. I noticed that while I was introducing myself, the man was staring at the stage with a stricken expression. Before he even said hello or told me his name, he stabbed his finger in the direction of our band and said, "What is *that*?"

His indignant tone set off an alarm in my head, but I smiled and calmly said, "That's our worship team. We run through our songs every Sunday morning before the congregation starts arriving. We'll be done in about ten minutes."

He let out a puff of air. In a voice dripping with condemnation, he said, "We didn't come here to see a floor show. We came here to worship God."

Several smart-aleck one-liners came rushing to the front of my mind at that moment, begging to be fired back at the man's smug little face. (Among them was a comment about how, if he didn't like how our worship team makes music, he'd probably hate how our dancing girls serve Communion.) But you'll be happy to know I was good; I did *not* fall prey to what I freely admit was a devilish impulse. Instead, I politely asked the man not to judge us too quickly but to stay and worship with us and draw his conclusions when all was said and done. He said he would, but on the opening song—an up-tempo, jazzy arrangement of an old chorus—he grabbed his wife by the arm and stomped out. And I do mean stomped. He made sure his body language communicated to everyone around him that he was thoroughly disgusted.

Would you like to guess what that guy does for a living?

That's right; he's a preacher.

Trust me on this: just because the Joel Osteens of the world have popularized a nonthreatening, feel-good style of preaching doesn't mean the guiltmongers aren't still out there. They're piloting churches all across the country, spewing poison from their pulpits and making decent, God-fearing people feel guilty for just about everything they do—in spite of the fact that the word *gospel* means "*good* news," in spite of the fact that both Jesus and Paul warned us not to be judgmental, in spite of the fact that we're saved by grace and called to freedom in Christ, and in spite of the fact that Jesus said he came into the world to save it, not condemn it.

> Just because the Joel Osteens of the world have popularized a nonthreatening, feel-good style of preaching doesn't mean the guiltmongers aren't still out there.

Guiltmongers always make me think of H. L. Mencken's famous definition of Puritanism: "The haunting fear that someone, somewhere, may be happy."[2]

WHY GUILTMONGERS AREN'T EXTINCT

The question is, Why haven't these hammer-men gone the way of the dinosaur, the pet rock, and the leisure suit? Logic would tell us that any preacher who specializes in browbeating people would eventually find himself preaching to a room full of empty seats, thus necessitating a career change. But the truth is that these guys always seem to have an audience. There are three reasons why.

They Seem to Be Bible Experts

Every hammer-man I've ever known has been a Scripture-quoting machine. And in a world where so many preachers have all but abandoned the Word in favor of pop psychology, this can be very attractive . . . and very deceptive. A Bible-quoting preacher sounds like he knows what he's talking about. People have a tendency to believe him because he's constantly backing up everything he says with a Bible verse. Those verses may be misapplied or twisted while other relevant verses are conveniently omitted, but most listeners won't be biblically savvy enough to realize it. I've heard many say in defense of their hammer-man pastor, "He may not be the best preacher in the world, but he really knows his Bible," as if his ability to quote Bible verses is the only thing that matters to them.

They Have a Commanding Presence

All the hammer-men I've ever known have had big, booming voices and strong personalities. When you're in their presence, everything seems under control. And it is—under *their* control, which may not be a good thing in God's eyes but is perfectly OK with people who are subservient by nature. They like the idea of someone else doing all the thinking and calling all the shots.

They Meet the Felt Need Some People Have to Be Punished for Their Sins

Many of us are like the character in a movie I watched recently. He betrayed a friend and felt awful about it, so he begged his friend to punch him in the mouth to even the score. When his friend refused, he pleaded, "Come on. I deserve it. The world will never be in balance again until you pay me back for what I did to you." This is very similar to the mind-set a lot of people carry with them to church every Sunday. Their guilt feelings run so deep that a good tongue-lashing actually satisfies their sense of justice and makes them think the world is back in balance.

I'm going to be blunt right here.

If you attend a church where a hammer-man stands behind the pulpit—where you feel like you're being yelled at and talked down to and made to feel like there's something wrong with you if you don't happen to prefer the *King James Version* of the Bible—you need to find another place to worship. And that goes double if you struggle with guilt and inferiority to begin with. I don't care how many other good points your preacher may have, if he's a guiltmonger you're being hurt whether you realize it or not, and you need to leave. I know that's a disheartening thought, especially if you've been a part of the congregation for a long time and have friends there. The very idea of switching churches may make you sick. But you must face a cold reality: you will never find your way home from your guilt trip if you subject yourself to guilt-producing sermons week after week.

However, just leaving the church and finding another one isn't necessarily the answer either, since it's almost a certainty that you'll be pulled toward a similar kind of preaching. That's because you've probably been led to believe that any church that's not pounding the pulpit is shamefully liberal and soft on sin. So I want to spend the balance of this chapter talking about nontoxic preaching. You need to be able to identify preachers and preaching that truly honor God and edify his people.

GRACEMONGERS

Rather than being guiltmongers, preachers who truly reflect the heart and character of Christ are gracemongers. That's not to say they're soft on sin but simply that the default setting of their hearts is not condemnation. Gracemongers can denounce sin with the best of them, but like Jesus, their first impulse is to be understanding and kind, thoughtful and forgiving.

> Gracemongers can denounce sin with the best of them, but like Jesus, their first impulse is to be understanding and kind, thoughtful and forgiving.

The story of the woman caught in adultery (John 8:1-11) perfectly illustrates the difference in the two mind-sets. The woman found herself standing smack in between a group of bloodthirsty guiltmongers and the ultimate Gracemonger. The guiltmongers were itching to stone her. Not only was that their *first* impulse; it was their *only* impulse. With condemnation as their default setting, no other option even crossed their minds. But Jesus' first impulse was to give her another chance.

First impulses tell you a lot about a person. Given time to think and with a good PR manager to advise him, even a complete fool can eventually find his way to a benevolent position on just about any subject.

We've seen it a thousand times in the news. An athlete or celebrity impulsively says something outrageously offensive and then a day or two later "clarifies" his or her position after consulting with damage-control experts. The striking thing about Jesus is that he didn't need a PR firm. His first impulses were consistently gracious, his words consistently kind. This explains why he was known as the friend of sinners (Luke 7:34), why he hit it off so well with a woman who'd had five husbands (John 4:4-42), why he granted salvation to a hardened criminal (Luke 23:43), and why he prayed that God would forgive the Roman soldiers who were killing him (v. 34).

Oh yes, and it explains why the guiltmongers hated him.

When the default setting of your heart is condemnation, anything that smacks of grace looks like heresy.

Simply put, if you hope to make it home from your guilt trip, you need to find a church where a gracemonger stands behind the pulpit every Sunday. To assist you in your search, allow me to give you five characteristics of nontoxic preaching.

> **When the default setting of your heart is condemnation, anything that smacks of grace looks like heresy.**

Doctrinal Soundness

From the earliest days of the church, a premium has been placed on doctrinal accuracy. In fact, it was doctrinal *inaccuracy* that provoked some of the apostles' most strident warnings. Paul, for example, said, "Let God's curse fall on anyone, including us or even an angel from heaven, who preaches a different kind of Good News than the one we preached to you. I say again what we have said before: If anyone preaches any other Good News than the one you welcomed, let that person be cursed" (Galatians 1:8, 9). In a similar vein, the apostle John wrote, "If anyone adds anything to what is written here, God will add to that person the plagues described in this book. And if anyone removes any of the words from this book of prophecy, God will remove that person's share in the tree of life and in the holy city that are described in this book" (Revelation 22:18, 19).

Note the words starting with *A* in those statements:

- "Let God's curse fall on *anyone* . . . who preaches a different kind of Good News."
- "If *anyone* preaches *any* other Good News . . ."
- "If *anyone* adds *anything* to what is written here . . ."
- "If *anyone* removes *any* of the words from this book . . ."

There is absolutely no wiggle room here. God *demands* that anybody who preaches in his name must get the message right (or face the consequences). And to get the message right requires that you must be a serious student of the Scriptures.

I was in a young preacher's office one time. He was in his upper twenties and had been with his church about four years. I noticed that he had only about twenty books on his shelves. There were knick-knacks, picture frames, and keepsakes galore but only a few books. I, the quintessential bookaholic, commented on this, and he said, "I'm just not much of a book person."

Frankly, I would not sit and listen to that preacher week after week. I wouldn't sit and listen to *any* preacher that I know is not a book person, because that tells me he isn't a student. And if he isn't a student, then I can't trust him to be deeply into the Word. Instead, I would expect him to be pulling other preacher's sermons from the Internet and passing them off as his own. I would expect him to be regurgitating magazine articles and calling them sermons. It's one thing to use great ideas;

> In a world where false doctrines are flying around everywhere, a preacher needs to be a student if he's going to correctly explain God's Word.

all preachers do that. But stealing is not studying. In a world where false doctrines are flying around everywhere, a preacher needs to be a stdent if he's going to correctly explain God's Word (2 Timothy 3:16).

Theological Completeness

In Acts 20 we find Paul saying good-bye to the elders of the church in Ephesus. He'd ministered with them for three years. They had become close friends, but he knew he would never see them again. His emotional parting words contain this telling comment: "I declare today that I have been faithful. If anyone suffers eternal death, it's not my fault, for I didn't shrink from declaring all that God wants you to know" (vv. 26, 27).

This is one of my biggest complaints against the hammer-men out there slinging fire and brimstone week after week: they don't declare all that God wants his people to know.

They harp on sin. They rant about their pet peeves (such as using the wrong version of the Bible). They rave about how morality is free-falling in our culture. They demonize Hollywood and whatever godless celebrity happens to be making the news. They warn against God's judgment and the fires of Hell. But they don't talk enough about grace. The problem isn't that their preaching is inaccurate but that it is incomplete or, at best, out of balance.

Of course, it's possible to lean too far in the other direction as well. Many preachers—some of them very well known—are loathe to mention anything that might make their listeners uncomfortable. They steer clear of controversial topics and wouldn't preach a sermon on Hell if their lives depended on it.

The best way I know to keep the right balance in preaching is simply to preach Christ. Paul wrote to the Corinthians, "I didn't use lofty words and impressive wisdom to tell you God's secret plan. For I decided that while I was with you I would forget everything except Jesus Christ, the one who was crucified" (1 Corinthians 2:1, 2).

The great thing about preaching Christ is that, in him, you have the whole gospel in perfect balance. Take the cross, for example. It juxtaposes the hatred of man with the love of God. It puts sin and grace side by side. And how about the Sermon on the Mount? In it Jesus not only makes difficult demands but also offers tender encouragement. And in the stories of the Gospels we see Jesus befriending sinners and healing the sick while denouncing sin and calling for repentance. Anyone who preaches Jesus consistently will find himself preaching the whole counsel of God.

This doesn't mean every sermon has to come from the books of Matthew, Mark, Luke, or John. Every book of the Bible has a connection to Jesus. Every truth in the Bible is embodied in the one who claimed to *be* the truth (John 14:6). So whether the preacher's text comes from the Pentateuch, the prophets, or the epistles, his job is to find the connection to Jesus and help his listeners see it.

> **Anyone who preaches Jesus consistently will find himself preaching the whole counsel of God.**

Gracious Delivery

Again I direct your attention to a comment Charles Spurgeon made to his preaching students: "Excessively rapid speaking, tearing and raving into utter rant, is quite inexcusable; it is not, and never can be powerful, except with idiots, for it turns what should be an army of words into a mob."[3]

Consider also a comment from James S. Stewart, whom *Preaching* magazine named the greatest preacher of the twentieth century. In his classic work *Heralds of God*, he said: "Let yourself go occasionally if the Spirit moves you; but clamour is not necessarily inspiration, and shouting saves no souls."[4]

Finally, consider Paul's words to the Corinthians: "I came to you in weakness—timid and trembling. And my message and my preaching were very plain. Rather than using clever and persuasive speeches, I relied only on the power of the Holy Spirit" (1 Corinthians 2:3, 4).

These pulpit giants all seemed to believe in a gentle, gracious presentation of the gospel. They obviously preached with passion. I'm sure they raised and lowered their voices as the message dictated, just like a symphony contains many crescendos and pianissimos. But they weren't screamers. They weren't hammer-men . . . and neither was Jesus. Read the Sermon on the Mount and you'll find it almost impossible to picture him ranting and raving. We sense that he was under control at all times, even when he took on the Pharisees.

I heard a story once about a man who wanted to feed the pigeons in a park near his home. The first time he tried it he was very excited and went running toward the pigeons, slinging bread crumbs all over the place and shouting, "Here you go, little pigeons! Eat all you want! There's more bread where this came from!" But the terrified pigeons flew away.

The next day the man tried a different approach. He hid in the bushes until a pigeon wandered within reach; then he grabbed it and started stuffing food into its mouth, saying, "Here, this is good for you!" But again, the terrified pigeons flew away and the one he grabbed fought against him with all its might.

Finally, the man wised up. On the third day he took a seat on a park bench and sat there quietly, gently tossing bread crumbs onto the ground. The pigeons eventually decided the quiet man was no threat. Soon there were dozens of pigeons all around his feet, happily eating his bread crumbs.

Sadly, some preachers spend their entire lives yelling and screaming and trying to cram the gospel down people's throats. They seem to think that by cranking up the volume, waving their arms, and stalking back and forth across the platform they can add power to the gospel. But the gospel doesn't need that kind of help. Even at a whisper it is still sharper than any two-edged sword (Hebrews 4:12).

This great truth was reinforced in my mind when I actually did hear a man preach who could only whisper. Due to a paralyzed vocal cord, he was left with practically no voice. I heard him speak to a convention crowd of thousands. You could hear a pin drop as everyone listened intently. Many were deeply touched and said afterward it was one of the best sermons they'd ever heard.

Morally Challenging

When Jesus launched into the Sermon on the Mount (Matthew 5–7), I'm sure his listeners loved it. That first part where he talked about God comforting those who mourn and the meek inheriting the earth probably had them nodding appreciatively—the original chicken soup for the soul. But something tells me they weren't quite as tickled when Jesus finished with the chicken soup and started serving up castor oil. I'm referring, of course, to the hard parts of the sermon—like rejoicing when persecuted, plucking out your eyeball, turning the other cheek, and loving your enemies.

Jesus understood what wise preachers today understand: that good preaching challenges us to make changes in the way we live.

Occasionally, I am invited to speak to the preaching students at a local Bible college. One thing I always tell them is that every sermon is a failure that doesn't include a call to action. The sermon may be interesting, meticulously researched, and enlightening. It may start with the most hilarious joke ever told and end with the ultimate tear-jerker illustration. It may be a masterpiece of construction and flawlessly delivered, but if it doesn't call listeners to walk out the door and do something, it's a lousy sermon and a missed opportunity.

I'll even go so far as to say that if you're hearing great preaching week in and week out, you'll be called to do *hard* things. Gut-wrenching things. Things that you will not be able to accomplish unless you rely on God's help and strength. Again, I point to Jesus. In addition to the brutal challenges he laid down in the Sermon on the Mount, he also once asked a man to give away all his possessions (Luke 18:22) and another man, Peter, to forgive his enemy 490 times! (Matthew 18:22). Jesus challenged his hearers to do whatever was necessary to bring them closer to God. Great preachers today do no less.

> **Jesus challenged his hearers to do whatever was necessary to bring them closer to God. Great preachers today do no less.**

Emotionally Uplifting

I listed this quality last not because it's less important, but because "emotionally uplifting" only counts if a sermon meets all the other requirements first. Any halfway-decent public speaker can be emotionally uplifting if he doesn't have to condemn sin or challenge his listeners to do hard things. It's the truly great preachers who are able to combine all these qualities and do it week after week.

Recently, I attended a convention where the keynote speaker directed his comments to preachers and other church leaders. He flat nailed me on a couple of points. I felt very convicted and knew that I needed to make some adjustments, not just to my routine but also in my heart. But I didn't feel downtrodden or beat up. I didn't think God was mad at me. I didn't think I needed to turn in my resignation. I didn't decide I was a failure, which is saying something for a guy like me who struggles with guilt and inferiority. Somehow that preacher managed to show me my weakness, my need for improvement, yet inspire me at the same time. I actually walked out of that auditorium pumped up and itching to do better.

Doctrinally sound, theologically complete, graciously delivered, morally challenging, and emotionally uplifting—that is the kind of preaching you need if you hope to make it home from your guilt trip. If you're not getting it, you need to go looking for it, because continuing to sit in front of a poison pulpit week after week will make it hard, if not impossible, for you to ever truly know the joy of the Lord.

HEADING FOR HOME

1. How long have you attended your current church? How did you happen to end up there? What are its strengths and weaknesses?

2. Is the preaching you hear each week generally positive or negative in tone? Does it focus on relevant topics? Does it call you to action? Are you motivated and uplifted after listening to your preacher?

3. If you have an unsettled relationship with your preacher, can you think of anything you might have done (or failed to do) that might be the cause? What will you do that might help the situation?

4. Do you believe your current church experience makes it easier to be the person God wants you to be? If not, why are you still worshiping there?

5. If you are blessed to have a preacher or teacher who is a gracemonger, what could you do to show your appreciation?

IIIIIIII 9 IIIIIIII

DOING BETTER AND FEELING WORSE

Duty declares: "This is the thing to do!"
But, Self, I am so lenient with you.
—*Edgar Guest*

Many a long-faced Christian has come into my office with the same question. Generally, the question comes out something like this: "I've tried so hard to get my act together. I've acknowledged my weaknesses and admitted my bad habits. I've worked hard to overcome them and made significant progress. I'm not perfect by any means, but my friends all tell me they see a big difference in me. Yet for some reason I don't feel any different. In some ways I feel even worse, like all this hard work has been for nothing. What's wrong with me? How is it possible that I can be doing so much better and feeling so much worse?"

This question is rooted in a reasonable assumption. If sin brings heartache and pain but righteousness brings joy and peace, then we would expect any movement from the former to the latter to produce positive emotions, or at least better ones. David poured out his heart to the Lord in repentance over his sin with Bathsheba, and it's clear that he expected to feel better as a result: "Restore to me the joy of your salvation, and make me willing to obey you. Then I will teach your ways to rebels, and they will return to you. Forgive me for shedding blood, O God who saves; then I will joyfully sing of your forgiveness. Unseal my lips, O Lord, that my mouth may praise you" (Psalm 51:12-15).

So what are we to make of a situation where repentance doesn't lead to greater joy and peace? Maybe you're now in a situation where guilt continues to hound you even though you've worked hard to become a better person. My guess is that you are making a very common mistake: concentrating all your energy on correcting the things you've been doing wrong but failing to deal with the things you *haven't* been doing at all. In other words, you've made good progress on your sins of *commission*, but you've ignored your sins of *omission*.

James warned against this mistake when he said, "Remember, it is sin to know what you ought to do and then not to do it" (James 4:17). Clearly, he saw one type of sin as being just as serious as the other. Yet most of us still pour the majority, if not all, of our energy into correcting our sins of commission, which are more visible. If you can quit smoking or swearing or blowing your top, people will notice and start treating you with more respect. You might even get a promotion or finally be able to get a date.

I remember reading an article many years ago that told of a man who had attached a dollar figure to several bad habits. Smoking, for example, not only requires money for cigarettes but also carries an invisible cost in terms of its negative stereotype and closed doors of opportunity. Many companies don't want to hire smokers because of the health risks, insurance costs, and diminished morale (smokers are notorious for their ability to annoy nonsmokers). So, according to the article, it's not just about the cost of the cigarettes. If you quit smoking, new doors swing open and your earning potential is significantly increased. And this is in addition to the fact that you'll be liked more if you're not stinking up every room or car you step into.

Without question, you need to be working on those noticeable sins of commission that so obviously cost you dearly—but never to the exclusion of other, less visible sins of omission. I have learned the hard way that sometimes it's the thing we're *not* doing that costs us the most.

Many years ago I lived in a wood-frame house with wood siding, heaven on earth for termites. I'm sure the message went out to termites all over the Southeast that my address was the mother of all buffet tables. This wouldn't have mattered if I had been diligent about getting termite inspections and treatments, but I hadn't been. I kept telling myself we could wait one more year and save that money. In the end I had to have one entire room of my house completely rebuilt at the cost of several thousand dollars, which was much more than it would have cost me to do the silly termite treatments.

Sometimes it's the thing you're *not* doing that costs you the most.

Right now, if you're doing better but feeling worse, I want you to swing the spotlight of honesty around and shine it into the dark corners of your heart. You may find a sin of omission hiding there, and it may be the very reason why, in spite of the improvements you've made, you still feel guilty.

> **Sometimes it's the thing we're *not* doing that costs us the most.**

To assist you in this process, allow me to ask you three questions.

IS THERE A PERSON YOU HAVEN'T FORGIVEN?

In chapter 7 I wrote about forgiving your critics. Here I want to focus on forgiving those who have harmed you in some other way.

No command of Scripture is more clear than the call to forgive. Paul said, "Get rid of all bitterness, rage, anger, harsh words, and slander, as well as all types of evil behavior. Instead, be kind to each other, tenderhearted, forgiving one another, just as God through Christ has forgiven you" (Ephesians 4:31, 32). And Jesus himself said, "If you forgive those who sin against you, your heavenly Father will forgive you. But if you refuse to forgive others, your Father will not forgive your sins" (Matthew 6:14, 15). There might be a lot of things in the Bible we can quibble about, but forgiveness isn't one of them.

But just because it's a clear, unmistakable command doesn't mean everybody does it. When it comes to forgiveness, I've noticed that people generally fall into one of five categories:

1. those who forgive

2. those who forgive conditionally

3. those who want to forgive but have a hard time doing it

4. those who have shoved aside thoughts of forgiveness

5. those who flat out refuse to forgive

It's the fourth group—those who have shoved aside thoughts of forgiveness—that I am primarily concerned about here. True, groups two, three, and five also have issues. Serious issues. But at least they're out front with their emotions. They're not trying to hide. Those who have shoved aside thoughts of forgiveness are a different story. They are living in denial, one of the worst things a person can do.

Several years ago I knew a woman who hadn't been to a doctor in over twenty years. She was a smart woman and knew the risk she was taking. She saw reports on the news about the importance of mammograms and Pap smears. She had friends whose lives were saved by the early detection of serious medical problems. Yet she shoved all those facts aside and chose not to think about them. I always believed that someday I would get a call telling me that she was having a sudden and serious health crisis, and I did. She didn't die, but she spent weeks in the hospital, much of it in intensive care. It took her almost a year to get back to normal. Interestingly, I learned that the crisis was triggered by her attempt to doctor herself with unwise amounts of over-the-counter pills.

I can't think of even one instance where living in denial of reality has turned out well. The reason, of course, is that word *reality*. If you're living in denial of some theory or hypothesis or possibility, that's one thing. But living in denial of *reality* plants the toe of the boot squarely on the seat of your pants. You can't hope to sneak past reality. It will get you every time.

> **I can't think of even one instance where living in denial of reality has turned out well.**

If your reality is that you have been deeply hurt and are harboring bitterness or hatred toward someone, you need to quit ignoring the issue and forgive. Doing so will help you in three important ways.

It Will Resolve a Conflict

Not the conflict between you and the person who hurt you; that may never be resolved. Rather, forgiving will resolve the conflict between your head and your heart. Your head, knowing what the Bible says, tells you that you need to forgive, while your heart, feeling the anger, says, "Not so fast!" It's like a tug-of-war going on in your spirit, and just because you try not to think about it doesn't mean it's not happening.

I once served a church plagued by internal strife. It was so discouraging to walk through the halls and see little groups with their heads together and know that they were plotting and scheming. Yet there were times when it was easy to forget what was going on behind the scenes. During the Sunday worship service, or if we had a concert or a special event, things seemed normal and even positive. But the conflict was always there.

And so it is with the conflict between your head and your heart. At times you'll be busy or distracted and won't think about it. But at other times (reading a book like this, for example) you'll sense its presence. Describing this feeling, a guy once told me that he felt like he had a rat in his head, gnawing on his brain. Forgiveness will kill the rat by resolving the conflict.

> A guy once told me that he felt like he had a rat in his head, gnawing on his brain. Forgiveness will kill the rat by resolving the conflict.

It Will Remove a Burden

Burdens are never good, which is why I have been known to buy two copies of several key books in my library, like the *New Living Translation* concordance that weighs approximately the same as an NFL offensive lineman. Even at $24.99, I still bought two copies. Why? Because I like to study at home in the evening sometimes and I didn't want to have to lug that behemoth back and forth. I just don't get a thrill out of carrying heavy things.

Imagine if we could actually see the burdens people carry. What if everybody had a backpack with all their worries and fears and unresolved issues stuffed inside? I'll bet if we could actually see them, we'd be amazed at the misery we put ourselves through and we'd get busy lightening our loads. And I'll bet there'd be a lot of forgiveness going on, because the burden of unresolved relationship anger is one of the heaviest.

It Will Reaffirm Your Identity

So you claim to be a Christian. Fine. But what if you don't do the things Christians are supposed to do? What if your life doesn't square with the teachings of the one whose name you so proudly wear? Wouldn't that cast some doubt on your claim, perhaps even in your own mind?

There was a time several years ago when I wasn't sure who I was. I was a son, a husband, a father, and a pastor. Then I became a writer, a new identity thrown into the mix. Then I became a grandfather, which complicated things even further. In those days I spent a lot of time thinking about who I was, because I knew the answer would determine my priorities. In the end I decided I am a Christian first and foremost. But in claiming that identity as the real me, I obligated myself to try my best to be Christlike. For me to willingly ignore my Lord's commands (such as the command to forgive) makes me look like an imposter.

So I'll ask you the question again: is there someone you haven't forgiven? You may have worked on your bad habits and improved yourself in significant ways, but if there's still unresolved conflict between your heart and mind, if you're still lugging a heavy burden around, and if you're still casting doubt upon your identity in Christ by refusing to obey one of his central teachings, it's no wonder you're still not feeling much better.

Is There an Area of Your Life You Haven't Surrendered?

Not far from the church where I preach, there is an old house belonging to a man who refuses to surrender to the changing landscape of our community. The house is on a tiny lot the size of a sticky note, completely surrounded by a four-lane highway in the front and a modern housing development on the other three sides. There used to be other old houses in the area, but their owners all sold out to the developer and moved elsewhere. I can only imagine how the developer must grind his teeth every time he drives by and sees that old house sitting there. It is an eyesore in the middle of what is otherwise a beautiful area, but even more so it is a testimony to stubbornness.

Sometimes I wonder if God doesn't grind his teeth when he looks at our lives and sees that, in spite of the improvements we've made, we still haven't surrendered one or two little chunks of spiritual real estate.

Years of service in the local church have taught me that many otherwise respectable Christians have refused to surrender their finances. Not only do they not tithe, they don't even come close. And then they get all huffy if the pastor dares to preach on stewardship.

Others refuse to surrender their pop-culture addictions. They sit in church and sing songs about holiness and sacrifice and then race home just in time to catch the *Sex and the City* marathon on cable. Or they pack their iPods with songs containing racy lyrics by artists who live the very smut they sing about. Or they spend more time reading gossip magazines and tabloids than they do the Bible.

> Sometimes I wonder if God doesn't grind his teeth when he looks at our lives and sees that...we still haven't surrendered one or two little chunks of spiritual real estate.

Still others refuse to surrender their nightly expedition into the world of Internet porn. In polite company they express outrage at the proliferation of filth in our society, but late at night, with the blinds pulled and the door locked, they surf cyberspace's red-light district like lust-filled sailors on a weekend pass.

I could go on. The point is that it's common for many Christians to stop short of full surrender. They're like an overweight guy who once said to me, "I can handle any diet you throw at me as long as it allows me to eat ice cream." But Jesus made it very clear that he expects his followers to surrender completely. Think about his words to a rich man concerned about his salvation. The fellow was a Goody

Two-Shoes if ever there was one, having obeyed all the commands of the law since his youth. But Jesus looked him square in the eye and said, "There is still one thing you haven't done" (Mark 10:17-21).

Or what about this stunning statement: "If you love your father or mother more than you love me, you are not worthy of being mine; or if you love your son or daughter more than me, you are not worthy of being mine" (Matthew 10:37). How's that for a blunt call to total commitment? Not even your parents—let alone something far less important—should be allowed to come between you and the Lord.

And then there are these unsettling words in the Sermon on the Mount: "On judgment day many will say to me, 'Lord! Lord! We prophesied in your name and cast out demons in your name and performed many miracles in your name.' But I will reply, 'I never knew you. Get away from me, you who break God's laws'" (Matthew 7:22, 23). The people Jesus describes here had some level of commitment. If they'd been prophesying and casting out demons, they weren't exactly gangster types. But they weren't totally committed, and that's Jesus' beef with them.

The question is, Why is Jesus so adamant about complete surrender? Is he just a hard-nosed party pooper who can't stand to see us have any fun? Cynics would probably say so, but look closely at this passage and you'll get a different answer: "Joyful are people of integrity, who follow the instructions of the LORD. Joyful are those who obey his laws and search for him with all their hearts. They do not compromise with evil, and they walk only in his paths" (Psalm 119:1-3).

Notice, first, that those described in this passage are indeed fully surrendered. They are people of integrity, searching for God with *all* their hearts, refusing to compromise, and walking *only* in his paths. But the point here is not just what these people are *doing*, it's what they're *getting*, and that is joy! Joy is one of the main by-products of an uncompromising commitment.

God's wish for all of us is not just that we wouldn't feel guilty when there's no reason to.

> **Joy is one of the main by-products of an uncompromising commitment.**

God's desire is much greater than that. He desires that we lead joy-filled lives.

That's why this question is so important. If you're doing better but feeling worse, if you've made some improvements but still haven't found the joy God has for you, it could be because there's still at least one area of your life that you haven't surrendered.

IS THERE A CALL YOU HAVEN'T ANSWERED?

God has been calling all kinds of people to serve him almost from the beginning of time. Abraham, for example, was a wealthy man; but Mary, the mother of Jesus, was a peasant girl. In social standing they were complete opposites, but God used them both.

Think about Samson and Timothy. Samson did amazing feats of strength that made him a real-life superhero. Timothy, on the other hand, was a sickly sort (1 Timothy 5:23). Two opposites, but both were called by God.

And not only does God call all kinds of people, he calls us in different ways. To Moses, he spoke out of a burning bush; to David, through a prophet. He spoke to Mary through an angel. To Mary's husband, Joseph, he spoke through a dream. To Philemon, he spoke through a letter.

I could go on, but you get the idea. God is in the calling business. Why wouldn't he be? He loves to partner with people in the working of his plan. From big shots like the patriarchs and apostles to peasants like the widow lady who dropped her mite into the offering basket (Mark 12:41-44), a long line of fascinating people have been called into God's service.

The question is, Are you being called to do something special for the Lord?

Before you say no, keep in mind that you're probably not going to hear an audible voice. Yes, God did speak audibly in Bible times, but that was before we had his Word in written form and before he sent his Holy Spirit into the world to guide us. In addition to his Word and the Holy Spirit, God can also move us toward our individual callings through the advice and counsel of godly people, through the alignment of circumstances, and through our own gifts and passions. All of these things can come together in harmony and give us a clear picture of what God wants us to do, without an audible voice being involved.

My point is simply that if God has placed a calling on your life and you have not responded, it could explain why, in spite of the improvements you've made, you still don't feel right.

Read the following Scripture carefully. "Today I have given you the choice between life and death, between blessings and curses. Now I call on heaven and earth to witness the choice you make. Oh, that you would choose life, so that you and your descendants might live! You can make this choice by loving the LORD your God, obeying him, and committing yourself firmly to him. This is the key to your life" (Deuteronomy 30:19, 20).

Anytime the Bible says "This is the key to your life," it behooves us to pay close attention. Specifically, Moses was telling the Israelites (and us) that the spiritual hat trick of loving God, obeying him, and being firmly committed to him is the key to life.

> **If God has placed a calling on your life and you have not responded, it could explain why, in spite of the improvements you've made, you still don't feel right.**

Obeying him is the tricky part.

The problem is that it's possible to obey the Lord's *commands* without obeying his *call*. You can follow all the rules, from telling the truth to tithing, but if you're not where God wants you to be, doing what he wants you to do, you're bound to feel at least a little unsettled, out of place, or even guilty.

Several years ago I saw this scenario played out in the life of a good friend. He was a strong Christian, he had a great family and a good job, and he was well liked. If ever a man should have been happy, he was the guy. But he wasn't, and the reason was that he'd felt God calling him to the ministry when he was younger but had chosen to pursue a more lucrative career path instead. He'd done well enough that anybody would have said God had blessed him, but he'd never been able to get past the feeling that he wasn't where God wanted him.

Eventually, with his career soaring, he walked away from it and went to Bible college. In one weekend he literally went from making great money to being a poor college student. He and his wife suddenly had to start making big sacrifices. She began working full-time and he worked part-time in between classes, often coming home dead tired to do homework. The hours were much longer and the pay was much less, but through it all he and his family found a level of joy that had escaped them before. He loved to say, "We've never been poorer and never been happier."

If you know in your heart that God is calling you to do something for him, I doubt that you're ever going to be totally happy until you do it. I'm not saying that God will chase you down and afflict you with storms and hardships the way he did Jonah, although he certainly has that prerogative. I do suspect, however, that he'll make it a point to keep reminding you of the work he needs you to do. Today it might be a song on the radio; tomorrow it might be a conversation at work; next Sunday it might be a point in the preacher's sermon. If God wants to remind you, he has no shortage of ways to do it. And in that constant reminding could be the reason why you're doing better and feeling worse.

> If you know in your heart that God is calling you to do something for him, I doubt that you're ever going to be totally happy until you do it.

Remember Screwtape, that legendary senior demon of C. S. Lewis's creation? When training his nephew and understudy, Wormwood, to be a conniving deceiver of men, Screwtape reminded him that the cumulative effect of little sins can work just as well as big sins.[1]

And what sins are smaller or less conspicuous than sins of omission? The word *omission* comes from the Latin word *omittere*, which means "to lay aside," hardly a definition that inspires visions of violence or vulgarity. Yet to lay aside something vital edges us just a little farther away from God. And if you edge far enough away from the one who is the light, you'll feel the absence of warmth.

If you've successfully dealt with your big sins but still don't feel like you thought you would, ask yourself a simple question:

What do I need to do that I haven't done?

HEADING FOR HOME

1. Have you been on a mission to correct some of your sinful habits? If so, what practical benefits have you seen? How do those results compare with what you were expecting?

2. Generally speaking, do you find it easy or difficult to forgive? Do you have an unresolved conflict with anyone? What has kept you from seeking a resolution? Are you willing to forgive that person here and now?

3. Is there secret sin in your life? If so, what does the fact that you keep it a secret say about both you and the sin? Are you willing to surrender that area of your life to the Lord?

4. Are you doing with your life what you always wanted to do? Are you working or serving in the area of your gifts and your passion? Is there something you believe God wants you to do that you haven't done yet? If so, why haven't you done it? How will you begin to move in that direction?

‖‖‖‖‖10‖‖‖‖‖

GOOD NEWS AND BAD NEWS

You are my refuge and my shield; your word is my source of hope.

—David (Psalm 119:114)

═══════════╫═══════════

Heard any good news–bad news jokes lately? Here's one I heard recently:

Lawyer: I have some good news and some bad news.
Client: Give me the bad news first.
Lawyer: Forensics has determined that the blood at the crime scene is yours.
Client: What's the good news?
Lawyer: They say your cholesterol is only 110.

As I wrap up this book, I am *not* joking when I tell you that I have good news and bad news. The good news is that you can come home from your guilt trip. If you've taken this book to heart, you may already *be* home, or at least a lot closer than you've been in a long time. The bad news is that getting home may well turn out to be the easy part. *Staying* home is likely to be the hard part.

Why?

Because you have an enemy determined to keep you from living a life of joy and peace. Satan knows your weaknesses and will use every means at his disposal to lure you right back into the toxic world of perfectionism, guilt, and inferiority. He'll make sure you notice all your peers who seem to be doing better than you are. He'll pass out fresh ammo to your firing squad. He'll turn up the volume on those voices that try to make you believe everything you do short of prayer and fasting is a sin. Above all, he'll try to diminish your thoughts of grace by making sure you see only Scary Jesus and not Suffering Jesus or Supreme Jesus (see chapter 2). And he'll do all of this with gusto because he knows these tactics worked on you before. He'll figure that if he just stays after you, you'll eventually let go of the things you've learned, start packing your bags, and take off on another guilt trip.

But you're going to have a little surprise for your enemy this time.

When he shows up, you're going to be ready. You're going to be protected by the one thing his bullets can't penetrate. You could call it spiritual Kevlar. Or you could just call it Scripture. Proverbs 30:5 says, "Every word of God proves true. He is a shield to all who come to him for protection."

Satan's helplessness against Scripture became obvious when he crafted a trio of insidious temptations to try to steal Jesus' integrity (Matthew 4:1-11). The confrontation happened in the barren Judean wilderness, prompting author Steven Lawson to call it "the original Desert Storm."[1] Satan wanted to undermine Jesus' mission on earth by disqualifying him as the Savior of the world. The confrontation was in the truest sense a winner-take-all contest. Second place is admirable in many competitions, but in this one it would mean total failure. If Jesus had lost this battle, we all would have been doomed.

But he didn't lose. He was able to ward off every temptation, and he did it with Scripture. Every time Satan spoke, Jesus deflected the deadly enticement with a simple statement that began with the words "The Scriptures say." He didn't preach a sermon or seize the opportunity to lay some heavy theology on the world. His Scripture quotations were short, sweet, and oh so effective. Picture somebody attacking a tank with a sack full of tennis balls, and you'll have a pretty good idea of the level of futility Satan experienced that day.

That's why I'm going to spend the last pages of this book sharing ten carefully chosen Scriptures with you. I believe God's Word will protect you the way it protected Jesus. When Satan shows up and tries to convince you to repack your bag and hit the road again, these are the Scripture shields that will enable you to deflect every temptation and counter every argument.

SCRIPTURE SHIELD #1: GALATIANS 5:1

"So Christ has truly set us free. Now make sure that you stay free, and don't get tied up again in slavery to the law."

Paul wrote these words to people who had accepted Christ but were allowing an extremist Jewish faction within the church (the Judaizers) to keep them tied to a long list of Jewish laws and traditions. The Judaizers believed that in order to be right with God, you had to both believe in Christ *and* obey the law. Paul said in essence, "No way. If you're in Christ, you're free from the law. Whatever you do, don't go back!"

In your life and mine, Satan will play the role of the Judaizers. When you leave all the anxieties and frustrations of your perfectionism behind . . . when you decide that you're not going to jump through anyone else's hoops anymore . . . when you decide that not everything short of prayer and fasting is a sin and that you're not going to constantly beat yourself up like you used to, you can bet Satan will show up and start whispering in your ear. He'll try to make you feel like a bad Christian by accusing you of lowering your standards and not trying as hard as you used to.

You'll be susceptible to Satan's arguments, just like the Galatians were susceptible to the Judaizers. Why? Because deep down you want to do the right thing. The fact that you're still reading this book tells me that you care about your spiritual life and relationship with God. It's all part of what makes you the good person you are, but it's also what makes you constantly afraid that you might not be doing everything you're supposed to do. It's what keeps you focused on rules and regulations instead of on God's grace.

Well, relax.

God is not calling you to slavery; he's calling you to freedom. He's not in the oppression business; he's in the liberation business. The last thing he wants is for you to believe Satan's lies and start packing your bags for another guilt trip. Now that you're home, make sure you stay home.

SCRIPTURE SHIELD #2: PSALM 103:13, 14

"The LORD is like a father to his children, tender and compassionate to those who fear him. For he knows how weak we are; he remembers we are only dust."

For a person who struggles with guilt and inferiority, these may be the most important verses in the Bible. I'm certain Satan seethes when he hears them because they expose one of his favorite lies—that God is a cruel taskmaster who is appalled by our weaknesses and failures.

Yes, I'm well aware that he uses the opposite lie too. I know there are times when he tries to defang and declaw God, turning the Lion of Judah into a big pussycat. But for the person who struggles with perfectionism, guilt, and inferiority, it's the fire-breathing, whip-cracking, lightning-bolt-throwing version of God that serves Satan's purposes so well. The last thing he wants is for people who are beating themselves up to realize that God is a tender and compassionate Father.

I especially like the statement that God remembers we are only dust. Of all household chores, dusting is the easiest because those itsy-bitsy particles are so wimpy. They show up by the millions like they've really got something going on. But when push comes to shove, they've got no spunk, no fight in them whatsoever. One swipe with one of those Swiffer doodads and they're history.

> For the person who struggles with perfectionism, guilt, and inferiority, it's the fire-breathing, whip-cracking, lightning-bolt-throwing version of God that serves Satan's purposes so well.

Doesn't it make you feel better to know that God hasn't forgotten what he made us from? We may act like we're made of steel, placing expectations on ourselves that only Clark Kent could measure up to. But God doesn't see steel when he looks at us; he sees dust. And what's even better is that he takes this into consideration when we mess up.

When my little granddaughter was being potty trained, not every one of her attempts was a complete success, but nobody cared. We didn't get mad. We didn't yell and scream at her if she had an accident, because we took into consideration that she was two years old. Yes, we continued to work with her and encourage her and raise expectations as we went along, but we understood that potty training is a process and we didn't expect perfection.

God is the same way. He never forgets that he's dealing with dust.

SCRIPTURE SHIELD #3: PSALM 27:4

"The one thing I ask of the LORD—the thing I seek most—is to live in the house of the LORD all the days of my life, delighting in the LORD's perfections and meditating in his Temple."

The Peabody Hotels are famous for their marching ducks. Twice a day the ducks waddle into the grand lobby and make their way down a red carpet to a beautiful fountain. One day I happened to be in the Orlando Peabody when the "duckmaster" was not able to keep his ducks in a row. One of the birds hung an unexpected left and meandered off through a large group of hotel guests who were in town for a book convention. People scattered, women shrieked, and the duckmaster took off in hot pursuit, which spooked the bird and made him even more flighty, no pun intended.

Marilyn and I were on the other side of the room, well away from the commotion, so for us it was mostly just good entertainment. I couldn't help thinking, though, that in life there's no such thing as keeping your ducks in a row. We perfectionists try. Oh, how we knock ourselves out in an effort to keep the little goomers perfectly lined up. But it's futile. That's why Satan loves to feed your perfectionist anxieties. He loves to sidle up to you and point out everything in your life that is zigging when it should be zagging. He knows that every wayward duck will drive you crazy and steal your joy.

> In life there's no such thing as keeping your ducks in a row.

That's why you need Psalm 27:4 to remind you that the only ducks that will ever be perfectly in a row are God's. Notice how David said that he wanted to spend his days "delighting in the LORD's perfections." David was smart enough to realize that he did not have any perfections to delight in, nor would he ever. And the same is true of you and me.

Do you see how this takes the pressure off? You no longer have to beat your brains out trying to achieve the impossible! The next time Satan criticizes the alignment of your ducks, tell him that since you're a child of God, his ducks are your ducks . . . and they are lined up just fine, thank you very much.

SCRIPTURE SHIELD #4: 2 TIMOTHY 1:7

"For God has not given us a spirit of fear and timidity, but of power, love, and self-discipline."

When the great jazz trumpeter Louis Armstrong was just a boy, his Aunt Haddie sent him down to the creek with a bucket to fetch some water. But as he was dipping up a bucketful, an alligator surfaced a few feet away, scaring him out of his wits and causing him to drop the bucket and run back to the house. His aunt told him to get back down there and not to worry about that old alligator. He's "just as scared of you as you are of it," she said. To which little Louis replied, "If that's the case, then that creek water ain't fit to drink."[2]

We can all name things we're afraid of, but we don't all live with a spirit of fear. A spirit of fear is a sense of dread that never goes away. It touches all the areas of your life, affects the decisions you make, limits your potential, and eventually begins to define you. Perfectionists have a spirit of fear. We're afraid we'll fail, afraid we'll be disrespected by our peers, afraid we'll disappoint people who believe in us, afraid we'll miss an opportunity, afraid someone might think we're lazy or incompetent, afraid the slightest little mistake will come back to haunt us, and on and on. The reason we perfectionists practically kill ourselves trying so hard is that we're trying to beat back a battalion of fears.

But God has not given us a spirit of fear!

What he *has* given us is a spirit of power, love, and self-discipline.

The difference is night and day. When you have a spirit of fear, you are being controlled. When you have a spirit of power, love, and self-discipline, you are *in* control. Satan understands the difference, which is why you can expect him to try to resurrect all your old fears even after you get home from your guilt trip. Don't let him do it. God has not given you a spirit of fear.

Scripture Shield #5: 2 Corinthians 12:9

"My grace is all you need. My power works best in weakness."

Two people can look at exactly the same thing and see something entirely different. Take tattoos, for example. Some people call them body art and think they're gorgeous—the bigger and the more detailed, the better. Others are disgusted by them and think that those who get them are weird.

Beauty is and forever will be in the eyes of the beholder, a fact that comes into play big time when we start thinking about guilt and inferiority. People who struggle with guilt and inferiority see weakness as an ugly, detestable thing; the ruination of their hopes and dreams; the thief of their happiness. But as Paul points out in this verse, God doesn't see it that way at all. He sees our weakness as a great opportunity for his power to do something amazing.

My wife and daughter love makeover shows. A time or two I've been walking through the room when they were watching one of these shows, and stopped to watch with them. I must admit it's amazing what those hair-and-makeup artists can do. A woman that you would call anything but pretty suddenly steps out from behind a curtain looking positively gorgeous. The audience gasps and applauds, dumbfounded at the transformation, while the artist beams with pride.

Paul's point here is that God is the ultimate makeover artist. Satan will condemn your weakness and make you want to beat yourself up. God will take your weakness and transform it into something beautiful.

Scripture Shield #6: 1 Samuel 16:7

"The LORD doesn't see things the way you see them. People judge by outward appearance, but the LORD looks at the heart."

The other evening I was fishing in Lake Atteberry (a retention pond behind my house). I had already reeled in a couple of nice bass, so I was feeling pretty good about myself. The only thing I was missing was one of those "Women Want Me, Fish Fear Me" T-shirts. Suddenly, the fishing equivalent of a frozen computer happened. When I threw my rod forward to make a cast, the lure splashed into the water about three feet in front of me. I monkeyed with the line for a moment, trying to pull the snag free, but it wouldn't budge. So I popped the face off my reel to have a closer look and was horrified to see the mother of all tangles. I've been fishing my whole life and have never seen such an ugly wad of fishing line. I have no idea how it got that bad without jamming up my reel sooner.

I didn't even attempt to untangle it. The only option was to cut it off and start over from scratch with some new line.

Perfectionists are a lot like fishing reels; we can look perfectly shipshape and shiny on the outside and be a tangled mess on the inside. Our friends and coworkers see how diligent and organized we are and assume that we have our act totally together. But if they could pop the face off the reel, they'd find a tangled, mangled mess. The constant obsession with keeping everything perfectly in order keeps the perfectionist's guts tangled up in knots, no matter how together he looks on the outside.

> **Perfectionists are a lot like fishing reels; we can look perfectly shipshape and shiny on the outside and be a tangled mess on the inside.**

That's why Satan's never-ending mantra to the perfectionist is, "Organization is everything!" Even after you get home from your guilt trip, he'll keep trying to lure you back into your obsession with things. But God says, "No, your heart is what matters. When you stand before me someday, the fact that your desk was never messy and your clothes were always pressed and your car was always washed is not going to count for anything. The only thing that will matter is your heart." Solomon affirmed this when he said, "Guard your heart above all else, for it determines the course of your life" (Proverbs 4:23).

When Satan starts whispering to you about how important it is to have everything in your life in apple pie order, remember: it's nice to have a clutter-free desk, but you can live a happy life without it. On the other hand, you *can't* live a happy life without a clutter-free heart.

SCRIPTURE SHIELD #7: MICAH 6:8

"The LORD has told you what is good, and this is what he requires of you: to do what is right, to love mercy, and to walk humbly with your God."

It's easy for us to get the wrong idea about God. For example, the Bible I've got lying open on my desk at this moment has 1,558 pages, not counting the maps in the back. And the print is tiny. And there are no pictures. I mean, we're talking about a ton of words here. The easiest thing in the world would be to assume that there must be a million things God expects. Otherwise, he would have just given us a brochure.

And boy, does Satan ever love to reinforce this notion, especially in the minds of those who battle perfectionism and struggle with guilt and inferiority. To us, life is already hard. Everything we look at seems to need fixing, and everything we do seems to be wrong. Add to that the notion that God's expectations are numbered like grains of sand on the seashore and you have the makings of a meltdown.

That's why this verse is important.

It explodes the myth that God's expectations are many and varied. According to Micah, God asks only three things of us: to do what is right, to love mercy, and to walk humbly with him. All those other verses in the Bible are there simply to help you do these three things. Mark this down and don't forget it: the Bible is intended to make your life easier, not harder.

> **The easiest thing in the world would be to assume that there must be a million things God expects. Otherwise, he would have just given us a brochure.**

So beware of Satan, the great complicator. He's the guy who took a simple command in the garden and twisted it around to make it sound like a secret conspiracy in order to steal a blessing from Adam and Eve.

Don't let him pull the same trick on you. Take your stand on Micah 6:8. Reject any way of life that is complicated and oppressive.

SCRIPTURE SHIELD #8: COLOSSIANS 3:23

"Work willingly at whatever you do, as though you were working for the Lord rather than for people."

Much of the guilt and inferiority we feel comes to us because we're trying to please people rather than God. The problem with pleasing people is that they're never satisfied, which is why you can expect Satan to do everything he can to lure you back into a people-pleasing mind-set. Whether it's your spouse or your boss or your parents or your coach or your customers, Satan will try to convince you that your success— even your worth as a person—depends on making them happy. Then he will sit back and laugh at you when you can't do it, and you end up believing you're a failure.

Paul's advice is simply to work for the Lord rather than people. Do what you do with one question in mind: What would Jesus think of this? In all likelihood, if Jesus would approve of what you're doing and how you're doing it, most people will too. Super Bowl–winning coach Tony Dungy is a good example of a guy who has lived his life to please only the Lord and found the adoration of people in the process. But even if people decide they don't like you, you can lay your head on your pillow at night and sleep like a baby, knowing that at least God approves of what you have done.

SCRIPTURE SHIELD #9: MATTHEW 5:20

"I warn you—unless your righteousness is better than the righteousness of the teachers of religious law and the Pharisees, you will never enter the Kingdom of Heaven!"

Be honest. As a Christian perfectionist, your goal is righteousness. You're not *trying* to be neurotic. You're not *trying* to be weird or difficult or hopelessly picky. You're not *trying* to drive yourself or everyone you love crazy. You're just trying to be righteous. That's why this verse should be of utmost interest to you. It's either good news or bad news, depending on how you look at it.

It's bad news—really bad news—in the sense that your righteousness will never exceed that of the Pharisees. Those guys were obsessed with keeping even the tiniest details of the law. They spent practically all of their waking hours studying the law that God gave and adding their own two cents' worth to tighten it up even more. Their hearts were far from God, but outwardly they walked the straight and narrow. You're not ever going to follow the rules better than they did.

On the other hand, this verse is good news—really good news—if you allow it to be what Jesus intended for it to be: an invitation to swap the chase after perfection for a simple relationship with him. He's saying, "Look, you'd have to be more righteous than the most righteous people in the world in order to *earn* salvation. So why don't you just give that up and walk with me day by day? We'll get through this thing called life together, one day at a time."

The next time Satan comes at you with that tired old line about you not being good enough, look him square in the eye and tell him that you no longer care about being good enough; you just want to be faithful.

SCRIPTURE SHIELD #10: TITUS 1:15

"Everything is pure to those whose hearts are pure. But nothing is pure to those who are corrupt and unbelieving."

One of the great joys of my life as a grandpa right now is watching *Barney* with a very short person sitting on my lap. Barney the purple dinosaur sings, prances, dances, and giggles while teaching lessons about love, friendship, sharing, and a host of other virtues that have become all too rare in our culture. Every time Barney and his friends break into song, Alyssa pulls me up out of my recliner so I can dance and do the motions with her. She's the only person in the world who could get me to do that.

I mention Barney because he has been quite controversial over the years. Perhaps you remember a group of religious zealots who tried to condemn Barney as being gay. They railed against him as if he were going to cause the fall of Western civilization and urged parents not to allow their kids to watch him. Because I wasn't a grandfather at the time, the controversy wasn't important to me. But now that I've seen Barney in action, I can only laugh and shake my head.

Paul was right on the money when he said that to some people absolutely nothing is pure. They'll tell you that not only is Barney gay, he might well be the antichrist. That is, if George Bush isn't the antichrist. Or Bill Gates. Or Barack Obama. This crowd will boo Santa Claus and protest Girl Scout cookies for not matching the nutritional content of a stalk of broccoli. Oh, and if you even think about driving a foreign car, they'll label you un-American.

I hate to tell you this, but if you make it home from your guilt trip, Satan is probably going to round up a battalion of these hypercritical maniacs and steer them in your direction. He'll try to fill your ears with condemning voices in an effort to undo the progress you've made. When that happens, your challenge is to remember what Paul said: everything is pure to those whose hearts are pure. That means that if you encounter someone who is always finding fault with everything you do, that person is not pure and you need to limit your contact with him or her. A person who *is* pure will be positive and encouraging and won't be constantly criticizing you.

Back in 1995–96 a seven-year-old girl named Chelsey Thomas made national headlines when she had surgery to correct a condition called Moebius syndrome.[3]

The condition is very rare, affecting only about one thousand people in the United States at any one time. Simply put, little Chelsey was born without the nerves needed to smile. The condition isn't fatal and it doesn't hurt, but anyone going through life with a perpetually sad expression is bound to face a host of social, emotional, and psychological challenges.

The delicate surgery had to be done in two stages, first one side of Chelsey's face and then the other side several months later. For each side doctors worked for eleven hours, removing a nerve from Chelsey's leg and inserting it into her face.

I'm thankful that Moebius syndrome can be fixed . . . that people who *can't* smile can be given the ability. But even when we *have the ability to* smile, we still need a reason. That's been the whole point of this book, to give hope to the millions of people who have all the nerves they need but none of the reasons.

If you've been traveling in the far country of perfectionism, guilt, and inferiority, and are just now arriving home, let me be the first to welcome you. You're going to like it here in this wonderful land where people sleep well at night, feel good about themselves, and relish the joy of their salvation.

> **Even when we *have the ability to* smile, we still need a reason.**

Oh, and by the way, that smile looks good on you.

HEADING FOR HOME

1. Having come to the end of this book, how much progress have you made in your battle against perfectionism, guilt, and inferiority? What significant differences can you point to that indicate progress? Is there a specific source of unjustified guilt that you have managed to let go of?

2. In the past, have you been susceptible to doubts and second thoughts when undertaking new paths and challenges? If so, is there a particular person who feeds those doubts? How will you deal with that person's negativity as you move forward?

3. If you were going to choose a theme verse for your life from this point forward—one to reflect your new outlook on life—what would it be? (It could be one of the ten listed in this chapter or one of your own choosing.)

NOTES

Chapter 1

Epigraph. Waylon Jennings, http://www.brainyquote.com/quotes/authors/w/waylon_jennings.html.

1. Rowe, Wordsworth, and Seneca quotes were taken from www.finestquotes.com and www.quotationsbook.com.

2. Waylon Jennings story details were taken from http://en.wikipedia.org/wiki/The_Day_the_Music_Died.

3. Michael Yaconelli, *Messy Spirituality* (Grand Rapids, MI: Zondervan, 2002), 45.

4. Mike Mason, *Champagne for the Soul* (Colorado Springs: WaterBrook, 2003), 52.

Chapter 2

Epigraph. Brennan Manning, *Above All* (Brentwood, TN: Integrity, 2003), 126.

1. Ken Gire, *The Divine Embrace* (Wheaton, IL: Tyndale, 2003), 62–63.

2. Philip Yancey, *The Jesus I Never Knew* (Grand Rapids, MI: Zondervan, 1995), 133.

3. Bruce Marchiano, *Jesus Wept* (West Monroe, LA: Howard, 2004), 17.

4. Ken Gire, *Moments with the Savior* (Grand Rapids, MI: Zondervan, 1998), 195–196.

5. Retold in my own words but based on James Bryan Smith, *Embracing the Love of God: The Path and Promise of Christian Life* (New York: HarperCollins, 1995), 165.

Chapter 3

Epigraph. Steve Brown, *A Scandalous Freedom* (West Monroe, LA: Howard, 2004), 53.

1. Anna Quindlen, *Being Perfect* (New York: Random House, 2005), 3–12.

2. Steve Brown, *Jumping Hurdles* (Grand Rapids, MI: Baker, 1997), 135–136.

3. Jonathon Lazear, *The Man Who Mistook His Job for a Life: A Chronic Overachiever Finds the Way Home* (New York: Crown, 2001), 89.

4. Miriam Elliott and Susan Meltsner, *The Perfectionist Predicament* (New York: William Morrow, 1991), 230.

Chapter 4

Epigraph. Tom Hovestol, *Extreme Righteousness: Seeing Ourselves in the Pharisees* (Chicago: Moody, 1997), 20.

Chapter 5

1. Winston Churchill, http://quotes.wordpress.com/2006/09/29/never-give-up-quotes/.

2. Steve and Mary Farrar, *Overcoming Overload* (Sisters, OR: Multnomah, 2003), 33.

3. Lin Yutang. Quoted by Jill Murphy Long, *Permission to Nap: Taking Time to Restore Your Spirit* (Naperville, IL: Sourcebooks, 2002), 6.

4. Clifton Fadiman and André Bernard, eds., *Bartlett's Book of Anecdotes* (New York: Little, Brown and Company, 2000), 267.

Chapter 6

Epigraph. Stephen Arterburn and Jack Felton, *More Jesus, Less Religion* (Colorado Springs: Waterbrook, 2000), 65.

1. Romi Lassally, *True Mom Confessions: Real Moms Get Real* (New York: Penguin, Berkley Publishing Group, 2009), 11, 18, 44, 63, 65, 84.

Chapter 7

Epigraph. Real Live Preacher, http://www.quotationspage.com/quote/31381.html.

1. Steve Brown, *Jumping Hurdles* (Grand Rapids, MI: Baker, 1997), 128.

2. Jim McGuiggan, *Jesus, Hero of Thy Soul: Impressions Left by the Savior's Touch* (West Monroe, LA: Howard, 1998), 19–20.

3. John C. Maxwell, *Winning with People: Discover the People Principles That Work for You Every Time* (Nashville, TN: Thomas Nelson, 2004), 225.

Chapter 8

Epigraph. John Selden, http://www.great-quotes.com/quotes/category/Preachers_And_Preaching.htm.

1. C. H. Spurgeon, *Lectures to My Students: Complete & Unabridged* (Grand Rapids, MI: Zondervan, 1979), 291. Can be seen at www.books.google.com.

2. H. L. Mencken, http://www.quotationspage.com/quotes/H._L._Mencken/31.

3. Spurgeon, *Lectures to My Students*, 115.

4. James S. Stewart, *Heralds of God* (Grand Rapids, MI: Baker, 1972), 184. See also http://www.preaching.com/resources/past_masters/11557530/James%20S.%20Stewart/.

Chapter 9

Epigraph. Edgar Guest, from the poem "Dealing With Me" in *The Light of Faith* (Chicago: Reilly & Lee, 1926), 130.

1. C. S. Lewis, *The Screwtape Letters*, rev. paperback ed. (New York: Macmillan Publishing, Collier Books, 1982), 56.

Chapter 10

1. Steven J. Lawson, *Faith Under Fire* (Wheaton, IL: Crossway, 1995), xii.

2. As told by Max Lucado, *Come Thirsty* (Nashville, TN: W Publishing Group, 2004), 144–145.

3. "Girl's Surgery Is Performed for a Smile, Doctors Hope," http://www.nytimes.com/1995/12/16/us/girl-s-surgery-is-performed-for-a-smile-doctors-hope.html (accessed December 9, 2009).

═══ A MESSAGE FROM MARK ═══

Dear Reader,

Thank you for the time you have given to reading this book. If you're a first-time reader of my work, welcome to my world. If we've met before in the pages of other books, thank you for continuing to support my writing ministry.

Because the publisher and I understand what an ongoing struggle it can be to overcome guilt, inferiority, and perfectionism, we have set up a special Web site:

www.ComeHomeFromYourGuiltTrip.com

Feel free to stop by on a regular basis. I will be posting blog entries designed to give you support and encouragement. You can also share your own thoughts to help others traveling the same road.

If you'd like to contact me personally, my e-mail address is MarkAtteberry@aol.com, and I am on Facebook.

In Christ,
Mark

OTHER BOOKS BY MARK ATTEBERRY

So Much More Than Sexy
Free Refill
The 10 Dumbest Things Christians Do
Walking with God on the Road You Never Wanted to Travel
The Caleb Quest
The Climb of Your Life
The Samson Syndrome

WEB PRESENCE

MarkAtteberry.net
SoMuchMoreThanSexy.com
ComeHomeFromYourGuiltTrip.com
Facebook

Living with an **unforgiving** heart is like living with a **gorilla**

An unforgiving heart ruins relationships, affecting everyone and everything you touch. Maybe you've tried and failed to forgive someone who's hurt you. Maybe you aren't sure you even *want* to try.

In these confessions from Brian Jones's own struggle, find hope and strength for finally getting rid of the gorilla in your life.

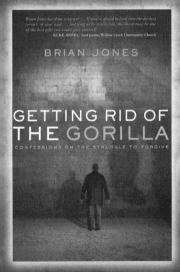

Item # 24335

Explore the struggle to forgive with a small group using the Group Member Discussion Guide
Item # 41184

Visit at your local bookstore or www.standardpub.com